GREAT IDEA! NOW WHAT?

Howard Bronson and Peter Lange

Small Business Sourcebooks

from **Sourcebooks** Inc.

Naperville, Illinois

Published by: **Sourcebooks, Inc.**
P.O. Box 372, Naperville, Illinois, 60566
(708) 961-3900
FAX: 708-961-2168

Editorial: Todd Stocke
Cover Design: Wayne Johnson/Dominique Raccah
Interior Design and Production: Andrew Sardina, Sourcebooks, Inc. and Peter Lange

This publication is designed to provide accurate and authoritative information in regard to the subject matter covered. It is sold with the understanding that the publisher is not engaged in rendering legal, accounting, or other professional service. If legal advice or other expert assistance is required, the services of a competent professional person should be sought.
From a Declaration of Principles Jointly Adopted by a Committee of the American Bar Association and a Committee of Publishers and Associations

The **Small Business Sourcebooks** series is designed to help you teach yourself the business essentials you need to be successful. All books in the series are available for bulk sales. Call us for information or a catalog. Other books in the series include:
- *Mancuso's Small Business Resource Guide*
- *The Internet Business Primer*
- *Your First Business Plan*
- *The Small Business Start-Up Guide*
- *The Small Business Legal Guide*
- *Getting Paid in Full*
- *Smart Hiring*
- *How to Get a Loan or Line of Credit*

Library of Congress Cataloging-in-Publication Data
Bronson, Howard F., 1953-
        Great idea! now what? : how to turn your idea, invention or business
venture into a moneymaking success / by Howard Bronson with Peter Lange.
            p.   cm. — (Small business sourcebooks)
        ISBN 1-57071-040-6 (hc.) : $17.95. — ISBN 1-57071-039-2 (pbk.) : $9.95
        1. New business enterprises. 2. Small business — Management.
3. Inventions — Marketing. I. Lange, Peter, 1964-   . II. Title. III. Series.
HD62.5.B76   1995
658.02'2 — dc20   95-11555
                                                                                        CIP

Printed and bound in the United States of America.

Paperback— 10 9 8 7 6 5 4 3 2

Table of Contents

Foreword

by Howard Bronson

"I've got an idea, but I don't know what to do about it. It's a good idea, but I just don't know where to begin."

Does the above thought describe you? Have you ever come up with a good idea, a new venture, a way to enhance either your small business or major corporation but then felt you'd never have the means to bring that concept to reality. Take heart! You're not alone. You're among the millions of people who have great inspirations every day. But then what happens? Pffft!—the dream dies, the world never realizes the benefit of that part of you, and you won't achieve your goal. After all, there's no benefit in dreaming unless you are willing to learn how to act upon those dreams.

The all new *Great Idea! Now What?* is designed to be your correct first step. For just the small price you paid for it, you have hired our experience; a consultancy that on a personal basis could cost you thousands of dollars. In essence, you are saying, *"Hey guys, I've hired you to help make the best out of the best of my idea!"* or more specifically, you invested in our abilities to help you profit from your ideas.

Great Idea! Now What? reflects years of learning and headaches that you'll never have to go through. For me, it all started with another book of mine entitled, *Good Idea! Now What?* I started from scratch and sold 50,000 books on my own before Time-Warner tracked me down and bought it. I learned in the trenches. Succeeding with that first book on my own was essential so I could prove to people like yourself that it could be done; that major marketing and development techniques I either created or discovered could be adapted for your own personal use; that $50,000 marketing and advertising campaigns could often be achieved with better results for just a few hundred dollars; and that effective, results-getting marketing concepts could be customized for your own particular needs. This book is a dream-preserver and nurturer of ideas large and small, laid out in a step-by-step fashion, complete with areas for you to notate and track your progress. It will become your own custom-guide—engineered by you, just for you.

When I first had the idea to write *Good Idea! Now What?*, I presented rough drafts to top-notch professionals in many fields. These ad execs, marketing consultants and other business pros all had the same passionate reaction. They hated it, and worse. They all felt the idea of starting or augmenting a business through free or almost free resources was unrealistic.

Well, I listened to all these passionately opinionated folks, but luckily I trusted my own instincts just a little more, believing that millions of dreamers were getting a raw deal, and that too many great ideas were dying unnecessarily.

Further, my book made it blatantly obvious that money was being wasted by people who just didn't realize that much of their marketing and development could be done for little or no money, people who were formerly spending ten or twenty thousand dollars for a limited radio or TV tour or for various print publicity campaigns that never produced results. Now those same people are achieving much better results while investing only a few hundred dollars or less.

The book continues to grow in new and exciting ways, with all kinds of new electronic support material in development. And I'm pleased to have a brilliant new research and writing partner in this new version. His name is Peter Lange, and he has helped to take *Good Idea! Now What?* into so many exciting new directions, increasing its value and power to you the reader. It has truly earned its new title *Great Idea! Now What?*

Through this book, we are first going to work together to cultivate the best idea for you to work with, and then take it step by vital step until it successfully reaches the end-user—the customer. To have that essential economic edge into the new millennium, you have to find the most practical way to build your dreams. It's our job to give your dream strength and integrity while helping you prove to yourself that the best marketing paths are often the least expensive.

There are so many things that you can do to bring your idea to life. Don't let it die—you have no excuses now. This book is your marketing conditioner. Be patient and flexible.

I am an avid mountain-biker and was having trouble pedaling up the steep rocky hills in my woods until I began picturing myself making it successfully to the top. Have the courage to have a vision greater than yourself, and let that vision sustain you.

So let's get started! First, not with a fancy or even a simple plan as many might try to convince you. As you'll see when you're finished, this book will become your master-planner research and development marketing guide. First, you must begin by making the following promise to yourself:

I, _____, have purchased Great Idea! Now What? to help make a positive difference in my life by helping me to bring my idea(s) to fruition. I realize that overnight success can take a year or longer, and that while there are no substitutions for hard work, there are usually better, quicker and far less expensive ways in which to channel my valuable time.

I recognize that no failure is a waste of my resources if I have learned to use that failure as a stepping stone and then found a way to move ahead— and that it's better to make a thousand mistakes on a small scale than one mistake on a larger scale. To this end, I shall temper my zealousness with good listening and positive, ongoing self-reevaluation.

I am keenly aware that while I may have a limited or even highly limited operating budget, I can still generate an unlimited amount of courage, enthusiasm and wisdom to see new opportunities every day. And I will be my own light, I will connect my own dots and find the right path to my success.

Signature	*Date*

Disclaimer

Dreaming can evoke wonder and great success. Dreaming can also evoke fear and frustration. Dreams are delicate, but if properly nurtured, can transform a mere notion into an industry.

Then why do some dreams fail? Why do so many great ideas never get the chance they should?

The primary reason is that most people are not aware of the many commonsense steps available to turn an idea into something viable. Most of these commonsense steps and techniques are either free or cost very little money.

The intention of this book is to advance as many ideas as possible by guiding people in cost-effective directions; ideas that people used to think they could not afford to develop. In designing this book, we attempted to prevent you from spending your money or energies in the wrong direction. We've made our best efforts with this new updated rendition and hope you'll do the same. Still, there are no guarantees for success. Some readers might make a lot of money or realize even loftier goals. Others may not. No book, seminar or program can responsibly guarantee your success. We cannot, but perhaps we can assist in your quest for advancement. The real success of your venture is up to you!

It's never the good dreams that fail; it's all in the choices the dreamers make.

How to Use This Book

The all new *Great Idea! Now What?* has been designed like a user-friendly computer, complete with cross-referencing and ready access to all the information you need when you need it. The goal is to provide you with all the appropriate resources and references to either enhance your existing ventures, or to start new ones, and then to bring those ventures to sustaining and profitable levels.

The book lays out ten principal activities that embody concept development as well as the turning of that concept into a business. These activities and their interrelationships are illustrated below:

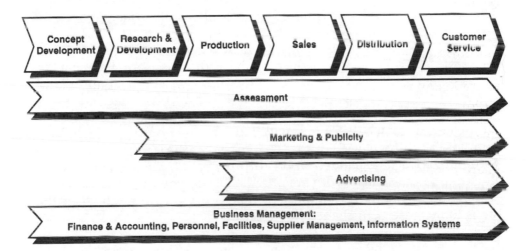

Each activity is presented in one or two chapters. The six activities across the top of the diagram and the "Assessment" activity just below these six constitute the primary concept development and delivery activities relative to the customer. These are the steps that add value to your initial *Great Idea* from the customer's perspective. The customer will ultimately be glad to pay you CASH for the value added in these activities. The remaining three activities are necessary to support your venture and make the customer aware of your *Great Idea*. All of these activities together can be thought of as the *Now What?* after your *Great*

Idea has surfaced from your incredible mind! This *Now What?* is exactly what we intend to show you how to do throughout this book.

The placement of the activities in the diagram indicate the relative sequence and overlap of activities. However, this is only a model. In reality, many activities can be underway all at once. Every project is unique and requires a flexible application of the basic model we are providing to you.

At the beginning of each chapter, the diagram shown on the previous page will be repeated with activities shaded relative to the chapter content. Each activity is also rated for degree of difficulty according to the following scale:

1 - Easy
2 - Slightly Challenging
3 - Moderately Challenging
4 - Challenging
5 - Very Challenging, but Definitely Possible

This information will be displayed graphically as illustrated above.

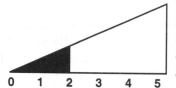

Each chapter will also begin with a list of *Action Steps* which will be discussed in the chapter. These are provided to give you a good idea of where we are going before you get started.

At the end of each chapter, you will find three sections which will help you "put it all together" for that chapter. First, the *Action Steps* will be summarized and expanded upon to provide the details which were illustrated in the chapter. ❑'s are provided to for you to check off as you complete each item. It is important that you work through *all* of the steps to increase your chances for success.

Second, some of the more common challenges which people like yourself face when undertaking the chapter will be identified. Solutions for dealing with each of these challenges are provided. You should note that even though we are providing you with this information in hopes that you will learn from others, you will experience your own learning process and will more than likely have to learn your own lessons.

Finally, we do NOT want you to continue until you can affirmatively answer the questions at the end of each chapter. If you cannot answer affirmatively to every question, DO NOT continue with the next chapter. Your ultimate success will depend on your ability to replicate our

Action Steps which have proven successful countless times. Again, ❑'s are provided to for you to check off as you affirmatively answer each question.

Tips, Exercises and Stories

To facilitate your adventure, we have added tips, exercises, and stories. Each of these items are designated by specific icons as follows:

 "Power-Up Tips" are designated by electrical plugs. These are helpful tidbits that you can plug into your *Great Idea* for a burst of energy.

 Exercises or "Connections," designated by electrical outlets, are your opportunities to plug into the power of this book. "Connections" contain all necessary concept assessment and development forms to help insure structure and growth for your *Great Idea*. These exercises will help you focus in on the ideal concepts and strategies.

 The "Scrapbook" icon designates relevant stories or anecdotes from either Lange or Bronson. These are stories which we believe are beneficial to the development of your concept.

Time is tighter these days, so reference books of this nature have to deliver more information in more efficient ways. It is our hope that we have created a workable format that integrates well with your lifestyle and delivers the results that you need.

Dedication

This book is dedicated to you, the reader—to your adventure, your success, learning from your mistakes, and most importantly, to your vision. May this be the best $9.95 you ever spent.

Introduction

"If you have built castles in the air, your work need not be lost; that is where they should be. Now put the foundations under them."

Henry David Thoreau

Every Tuesday at Twelve Noon, The U.S. Patent Office in Arlington, Virginia issues over 2,000 patents to individuals or businesses. These original creations or improvements on existing ones could be a better chocolate-chip cookie or a system to power artificial hearts with a patient's own stomach acid.

That's a lot of patents each year, and that doesn't include the billions of inspirations that race in and out of our heads daily. And what about the thousands of business or community ventures begun each day? How many actually amount to something?

Think of the times you've had a great idea that died simply because you didn't know how easily you could turn that thought into profit. Most of us, even those who get to the patent stage, do not know how to bring our ideas successfully to market. One or two naive attempts and we sour on the whole process.

The idea fizzles out, and our productivity and hopes are diminished. Worst of all, the world never gets the benefit of what could have made life more productive, safer, more profitable or more enjoyable.

But there are many ways to make your ideas come to life, and they are neither expensive nor complicated. In fact, many of our high credibility production and advertising systems are virtually free. Well, actually there are a few minor expenses for hefty high-tech equipment such as pencils, stamps, clay, paper—things like that.

These are systems that work and have indeed worked for countless clients from Cape Cod to China. We have small Mom and Pop clients who have saved hundreds of dollars. We also have some big clients who have saved hundreds of thousands of dollars by adopting our systems.

Hundreds of people come to us each year with ideas, either in the dream stage or out of the patent office. As we're sure yours are, most of these ideas are wonderful and clever, and we've always wished we had the resources to develop all of them.

Because we don't have the time to help each of you personally, we decided the best way to reach you was through an information packed resource book designed specifically to advance your idea.

We will prove to you that you can do it inexpensively, but with a powerful degree of credibility and effectiveness. If you're an individual adventurist, this book is perfect for you because it will give you the development and exposure power without the big financial risk.

If you run a company or any type of organization, be it tiny, medium or ultra-large, we have a challenge for you: the next time you have a new product or service which you may want to develop and introduce to the public, have your agency employ our techniques as a test. The money you save could forever change the way you use the services of an ad or publicity agency.

Some of you will use this book to develop that artificial heart battery or that better chocolate-chip cookie (please hurry!). We have spent years researching and refining these techniques and now want to share them with you.

You will need spirit, patience and a good sense of humor. You will have to learn how to listen and then make your own final decisions.

We will take you step by step along a path that can make your dreams happen. Occasionally, you'll be subjected to a brief story from our experience (or sometimes seemingly from outer space) to help you understand a concept or avoid a costly mistake. If you're willing to live many of our stories vicariously, you can profit from our blunders and our successes without having to pay for them.

If this is your first venture, great. You've come to the right place. We'll show you how to exploit your imagination without exploiting your wallet. If you've been in any aspect of this business for a while, we hope our systems will compliment and enhance your existing skills.

The fact that many people who have already made it and have purchased this book to refine or streamline their techniques should come as encouraging news to those of you who are just starting out. No matter who you are, you're getting marketing information that's easy to follow, yet so effective, the pros use it.

You'll hear about successful people who perpetually praise the free-enterprise system. It's worked for them, and it can work just as beautifully for you, especially if you employ our techniques. There is no talent barrier here, and there are no limits. So don't impose any on yourself.

All anyone needs to begin is either a realistic dream or the willingness to explore the possibility of creating one. The realization of every person's dream is an American birthright, but the proper steps must be taken to profit from that dream.

So do you have to be a ruthless or legal thief to get rich on your ideas? Of course not, though there are many vultures on this earth. We're proud to count not one of these types as our friends.

Luck? Hard work? Dedication? Real estate? Inheritance? What's the formula?

Well, did you ever stop to think that after you've heard all those platitudes for success, you still haven't learned a thing about personal success? Until you jump in the game, you won't.

Statistics indicate that more than half of you have purchased some type of "How To Succeed" book at some point in your life. And what about those seminars that seemed so promising at the time, but ended up only leaving you a few hundred dollars poorer? Statistics also show that most books and programs don't deliver what they promise. So, we have really got our work cut out for us.

We've read many of the management, marketing and real estate "How To's." In our humble opinion, we think you bought the right one because we don't just throw you a few tips and expect you to create miracles. We, in fact, help you evolve your venture with solid systems for your success while also maintaining a sensitivity to your fears of success.

Our job is to team up with your imagination and make your idea sell. We are unconventional, and we reserve the right to break some of our own rules in the name of venture success. We hope you will break some of our rules when you find it necessary. We'll be with you step by step, chapter by chapter. If you stumble, get up and try again. If you can learn what made you fall, you can continue to grow with your dreams.

As time passes,
I get up,
And I fall.
I get up and I fall.
Each time, growing closer to success,
Flat face and all.

—From the book <u>Early Winter</u>
by Howard Bronson

Approach your project with courage and confidence no matter what the odds and no matter what anyone tells you. This book can be useful at any level. We don't care how ignorant or smart you are, unless you think you're too smart to take good advice. Our goal is to take your good idea, successfully make it grow and get it to the marketplace.

All we ask is that you stick with the book, not be discouraged and not let fears of failure close you down to the success you deserve and the success you will have.

Remember that any great civilization is based upon individuals' abilities to bring their ideas to life. Forget what you read five years ago or even last year; the entrepreneurial movement has just barely begun. As you will soon discover, hundreds of new developmental, promotional and sales avenues are created each day. It is our job to show you where they are and how to use them. You could be a Ph.D. or a high school graduate. It doesn't matter. The real secret to success is finding your own appropriate personal blend of wisdom and courage, and not necessarily in that order.

You've spent your hard-earned money for this book, so you want to get your money's worth. We've spent a combined total of over thirty years learning about you and what you need to bring your ideas to a profitable stage.

First, let us tell you what we've learned about you. While you don't believe in miracles, you know with the proper preparedness, timing and sometimes a little luck, you can make miraculous things happen. You know you are willing to work hard, but don't want to waste your energy, or most especially, your money by heading in the wrong direction. You have a great deal of dedication, hope, belief and fear about your idea. Your fears, by the way, are often justified. After all, confidence and dedication can only do so much. You have bills to pay and a concept to build, so whatever your financial situation, you don't have money to waste. No one does. But allow us to show you how your imagination and initiative will permit you to afford more than you ever dreamed possible.

We share your concerns and want your idea to become successful. In fact, we've spent much of our marketing and consulting careers helping people realize and develop their own potential—from NASA to Peter Rabbit. It has not always been easy. We have struggled with many concepts and programs, always with one basic overall belief—we never gave up on a good idea as we helped people to discover the best of their potential.

Now we're major business and marketing consultants. From chocolate-chips to micro-chips, we've been there, and we'll help you get there effectively and inexpensively. Without even knowing you, we already know your idea has potential. Oh, it might not end up just as you first envisioned; in fact, we'll guarantee that. Your concept may have to be reworked many times to accommodate the appropriate target market.

But we have made a careful study of the shortest distance to the successful creation and sale of an idea. That's why companies hire us, and that's the purpose of this marketing guide: to provide you with the most useful, the most important information you'll need to bring your idea to life.

It's all here and always growing, just like your venture; always getting better. All here: the same sophisticated techniques that major companies and organizations use on a large scale, rewritten exclusively for both the layman and the executive who wants to do it right. All the important names, complete with addresses, and all the steps and techniques you need to get your idea going in the right direction are laid out step by step for you. The venture-success information that we've dedicated much of our lives to uncovering is all here.

Use it well and learn how to celebrate the best of your potential with this guide—fully adapted and dedicated to you, the dreamer, the entrepreneur, or the upper or lower-level executive who is ready and willing to learn how to put foundations under their castles in the sky—because that's what the world is all about.

Here's a nice quote from Calvin Coolidge to start us off on the right foot.

> *"Press On!*
>
> *Nothing in the world can take the place of persistence. TALENT will not: Nothing is more common than unsuccessful men with talent. GENIUS will not: Unrewarded genius is almost a proverb. EDUCATION alone will not: The world is full of educated derelicts. PERSISTENCE and DETERMINATION alone are omnipotent."*
>
> Calvin Coolidge

Chapter One

Finding Your Best Idea
The Process of Self-Understanding

> *"We are what we think. All that we are arises with our thoughts. With our thoughts we make the world."*
>
> **Buddha**

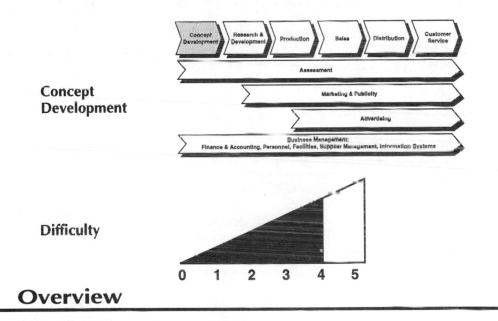

Concept Development

Difficulty

Overview

Too many of us often stumble into careers, families and general lifestyles, which even if secure and financially remunerative, stray us from a truer and far more profitable direction. Do you want to direct and act upon your life, or simply react to it?

This chapter provides the initial stepping stones for directing and acting upon your life.

Action Steps

1) Perform self-assessment of current direction.
2) Explore new potential directions.
3) Formulate a more fulfilling, and eventually more profitable venture.

The Caribbean night sky was bleeding stars. I had just finished an exhausting stint writing and producing radio ads for the American Express "Do You Know Me" account, so I was readily exhilarated by the cozy peace of this island.

Bronson

It was easy to hire a fisherman to take my date and I on a night cruise aboard his tiny boat. The stars cast a silver glow over the water, but it wasn't enough for us to see that piece of shark net out of place. The little boat jerked to an abrupt halt as its motor snagged on the net.

The sharks gathering around the boat seemed even more thrilled than I was since we must have looked very appetizing. We couldn't move, couldn't get the engine free, and couldn't row because we forgot the oars. It was Hell in paradise, and I pushed us into it. Just as my date was pledging to kill me if the sharks didn't eat us first, another small boat appeared in the night. "Are you where you wanna be?" the islander asked.

Oh sure we were. My date just loved being stuck with hungry sharks.

1) Perform Self-Assessment of Current Direction

Are you where *you* want to be? That's our first task, and it is the most important.

"I have a great idea!" Lightbulb flashing over your head, eyes as big as tomatoes. Everyone's had some kind of inspiration in their lives, but the trick is to keep that lightbulb burning bright.

If you already have your heart set on an idea, let's take a closer look at it to make sure you'll want to stay with it. If you don't have an idea in mind yet, that's fine. We'll take a closer look at how we all develop ideas and open ourselves up to the process.

From the beginning, you must promise never to limit your imagination. Maybe you've had a few brainstorms in your life. Maybe not, and at this point you don't know if you have anything you can really develop and market.

We can tell you that everyone has some gift that they can market successfully. Is it that special cake or little tool you make for neighbors? Is it your talent for solving conflicts or an idea to make your community a better place in which to live? It's there. You just have to recognize what you've always had, and then couple it with the processes outlined in the next two chapters.

2) Explore Potential New Directions

Creativity is the exploration of possibilities. You have to learn to play a game of "what-ifs" and play it to the max. If you're not willing to take the simple mental risk of astounding and shocking yourself, you run the risk of never really surprising or delighting yourself, never growing and never profiting financially.

There are many books that will attempt to offer you specific categories and systems to help you define your talents. We find this practice horribly limiting. One of our greatest reasons for our successes is that we never let anyone corral us into just one specific area.

We have earned a certain degree of freedom and control over our lives and you can have the same privilege as you learn to celebrate your personal potential and initiative. This is a free country. Don't be anyone's slave.

If your idea doesn't begin to gel after the first chapter, put this book down and don't continue until you have one that you really want to work with. That may take a few days or months. The delay makes no difference unless you're under a killer deadline.

In 1983 and 84, I was involved in the marketing of all the officially licensed Olympic products. My 20 Olympic product accounts each had firm time frames for selling. The day after the Olympics, most of these products (with the exception of some collectibles) were obsolete.

What an accelerated marketing education that was! I had to find markets in a very compressed time frame. I should have gotten a gold medal for all the headaches I had to put up with. I settled for the money instead.

I could tackle the Olympics because I had worked up to it, but I didn't start there. I started with individual products within reasonable time constraints, just as you will be doing.

Begin carrying a little notebook around with you and make notes about any ideas you may want to pursue. What are the dreams and wishes that make sense to your lifestyle? And you know those thoughts that breeze in and out of your head? Write them down.

Every spark counts when you are in the selection process. The human creative process seems to throw fragments your way as if from nowhere, and you find yourself almost automatically saying, "Nah, that's crazy."

From now on, when any of these notions whiz by, stop them in their tracks and write them down. Never say "Nah."

Every week or so, dump these notes on a table and try to see if some of these fragments are beginning to suggest an overall picture of what your venture may be.

Don't make copious notes, and there should be very little anxiety involved. Just gently plant a few seeds here and there, and keep checking for patterns. Look and listen in your own style. You're aiming to grow with something that's going to be an important part of "where you want to be."

Don't limit yourself just because you think a problem or goal seems a bit large in scope. Writing this book seemed scary to us until we began attacking it page by page, and one day we found ourselves with a book.

That process will happen with your idea. As your thoughts develop, you begin to get a strong sense of what you'll work with. Often people come up with ventures that outwardly seem to have no relevancy to their lives. Real wishes are often breakaway hidden loves that need to be properly guided.

Too busy, lazy, sick, whatever. That makes no difference because the right idea will spark ample motivation. Hang up your hang-ups and take advantage of that incredible American gift of free thought and exploration. Many people have never allowed themselves to have a free thought in their lives, but it's so easy to learn how. Let your mind wander. You can always come back.

Go out and live your life as you normally do. Start off by simply thinking about possibilities. In no time, you'll find that you have more ideas than you ever gave yourself credit for. That discovery generally comes as a refreshing and motivating surprise.

Keep at it until you have really found something that you will nurture and market, something that you can grow with. Remember, if it is "Where you want to be," you'll find the wherewithal to stay with it.

3) Formulate a More Fulfilling, and Eventually More Profitable Venture

To continue shaping your idea, let's make a three-stage wish. Real wishes usually come true, but you have to know how to make a real wish.

Stage 1 - Hope / Belief: If we asked most of you to make any wish, most of you would wish for lots of money. Most people are indeed stuck in the first stage.

We have nothing against lotteries. In fact, maybe our income taxes should be replaced with mandatory lotteries. But "Lottery People" who hope that some freak remote chance will drape them in clover, rarely succeed. One must get past the first stage, because hope alone won't produce our success.

Stage 2 - Desire / Intention: This stage of our wish is that thing we want to improve, that problem that we want to attack. What specific area of your world would you like to improve?

Maybe you want to communicate better with your family or find a way to realize increased employee productivity? Maybe you want to develop a new or improved product or service? What about a way to do your small part to make the world safer for children? Let's work with the "safer children" notion as Stage 2 of our wish.

Stage 3 - Creation / Action:

Following is an actual example of how one of my clients brought "safer children"  *to the third stage.*

A rather brilliant man presented his concept to me by first telling a story about a girl he knew who dove into a swimming pool and was instantly electrocuted due to a frayed wire in an underwater pool switch. He vowed that he would muster his gifts to make sure such a nightmare would never happen again.

He channeled his passion into the development of an underwater safety switch that eliminated electrical contact near the pool area. The product he created and I marketed represents the vital Stage 3 of our wish and that's what you want to head to.

Be it a product or service, Stage 3 represents your rough plan of attack. This is one of the most difficult and pivotal points in developing a viable concept essentially because you have to often violate one key rule about human nature: safety. But the best time to risk all is when you are exploring the choice of the concept. It's safe because the risk is cerebral, and the better your self-exploration at this point, the better the chance for financial success, independence, and career fulfillment.

Connection #1
Creating a Mission
Statement

> *"When you get to the top of the mountain, keep climbing."*
> **Anonymous**

Good vision requires focus, and focus is the rudder that steers us toward our goal. But what is a goal, really?

A goal is more than just a target, it is a moving target. So, it's important not to be excessively rigid, because as your concept develops, it will change and grow with all the new pieces of data that you collect. The viability of your ultimate result will be contingent upon your own ability to best incorporate the many discoveries you make along the way.

Your First Task

In just one sentence, write your mission statement. What are you trying to do? What do you see yourself achieving? Begin the sentence with the word 'To.' Underneath your statement, write the following: 'Subject to change—A Lot.'

> *To...*
>
> **Subject to change—A Lot**

Now, put it up on the wall where you work so you can see it every day.

When we create mission statements, within a very short time they look very worked over, with original statements modified over and over again.

If it helps, make a visiual collage of your mission. Cut out pictures from magazines or do your own drawings. Paste them on a poster board along with your mission statement, and hang the whole thing on the wall.

The beauty of writing and visual graphics is that they aid us in sustaining our vision. So, get that mission statement on the wall.

Now get back to work.

Summary

Many of our readers already have their ideas in mind and are simply using this book as a market-reference, but our experience shows us that the best marketing, even the most money, won't sustain a poorly chosen idea. This is your life. Give it the value you want it to have!

1) Perform Self-Assessment of Current Direction

❏ Think about your likes and dislikes.

2) Explore Potential New Directions

❏ Begin to make notes about your random and fragmented thoughts.
   ❏ Carry a little notebook. 📖
   ❏ Write it down! ✍
❏ Periodically dump your ideas on the kitchen table and look for patterns in your thinking.
❏ Keep at it!

3) Formulate a More Fulfilling, and Eventually More Profitable Venture

❏ Make a three-stage wish:

Stage 1 - Hope / Belief
❏ Get past simply wishing for money, or becoming a wealthy vegetable.

Stage 2 - Desire / Intention
❏ Complete the following sentence: "I wish I could..."

❏ Complete Connection #1—Creating a Mission Statement.

Stage 3 - Creation / Action
❏ Use this book to turn that passion into reality.

Potential Challenges and Solutions

Challenge: "I don't see myself as an 'idea person.'"

Solution: This is the key problem. People have great ideas all the time, but without means of implementation; at least that's what they think. If you think of your ideas as dreams, you can achieve a better understanding. Dreams are the subconscious mind's way of digesting or processing old ideas and coming up with new ones. Listen to your dreams. They teach that we are all 'idea people.'

Challenge: "I don't feel I have what it takes to develop an idea."

Solution: The world cries out for improvement at every level, be it survival, leisure, etc.—you name it. One must get out in the world and try on a few idea hats to see how they fit. In this initial phase, it costs you nothing to mentally shop around for ideas, and in doing so, you will learn how to develop you own idea selection process.

Before You Continue...

❏ Are you taking a good look at what your true wishes are?
❏ Are you showing sufficient courage to explore your possibilities?
❏ Are you open to the possibility that your original idea may not be what you'll end up with?

Chapter Two

Advancing Your Concept
The Process of Self-Assessment

> *"If a man will begin with all certainties, he shall end in doubt; but if he will be content to begin with doubt, he shall end in certainties."*
>
> **Francis Bacon**

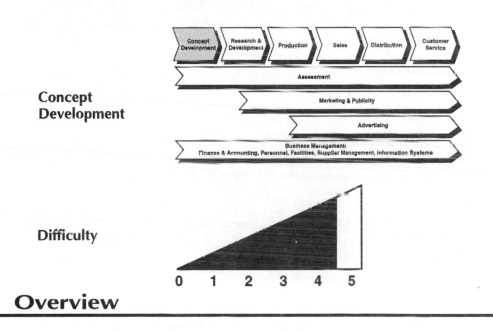

Overview

Having become more aware of what it really means to select the most appropriate idea, this chapter and its exercises will stimulate your thinking to help you focus on the concept that could best work for you.

Action Steps

1) Refine your self-understanding.
2) Determine your best idea.
3) Be open to new ways of thinking to make the best choices for your venture.

It makes no difference how simple or complicated your idea is. Everyone has the ability to act upon some idea that's personally important and/or just plain fun. Everyone we have ever met has some idea they want to develop and market. There has never been a more favorable climate than there is today for personal success. Coupled with our low-cost development and marketing systems, your personal possibilities are greater than ever.

This is not mere psychological cheerleading. Look at all the magazines and news items that now feature new products or services. There clearly is an increasingly receptive market for ideas from the individual dreamer, and we will show you the path of least resistance to get your share.

If you really want your idea to succeed, you must have a love affair with your idea, and falling in love takes some time. So take the time. No success in sixty seconds here.

When you finish with this book, we want you to have more than just gimmickry. We want you to have something of value that celebrates your personal initiative. That's where we want you to be. That's our Stage 3.

New Year's Eve 1995—most people are out getting sauced. Not me—I'm preparing to walk on fire! That's right. I decided that a fire walking seminar would be an excellent alternative to the usual cacophony.

The seminar leader guides us to midnight with three points of advice:
1. Be totally CLEAR about what you want.
2. Have an intense INTENTION to get it.
3. ACT in the face of FEAR to get what you want.

These three points are exactly what we want you to embody as you move forward.

My INTENTION is clear—get to the other side of the 12 foot path of 1200 degree coals without getting burned.

FEAR is present—anybody who has any sense at all knows that 1200 degree coals will badly burn your feet.

I ACT anyway because I have a CLEAR INTENTION—I walked not once, but six times!

That's a New Year's Eve celebration I will never forget!

Do you have your idea locked down? The right idea? If you think so, let's see if it will hold up through this chapter. But so far, you're doing great. If you're following our system, aside from the cost of this book, your only expenses so far have been for pencils and notepads, and you probably already had those.

"Is this all there is? Can I find my market niche? What is my potential anyway?"

Scary stuff. Do we matter? Do we have what it takes to make a difference and make a little extra or a lot of extra money in the process?

Of the thousands of people we have lectured or consulted, the above are the major concerns we hear over and over again with one important difference; they have taken the initial steps to *try* to make a difference. It is that *intent*, followed by *action*, that will make a difference in their respective ventures.

Even if you believe you have your idea all ready to go—just one step away from the market—do not skip this exercise, because the supporting theme of this chapter is to make *certain* that you have chosen your direction wisely and accurately. Very often, you will discover that your idea is right for you, that it is the best utilization of your personal resources. You may also just be playing with something that will ultimately bore you, even though you already picture yourself as that lucky fraction of a percent of those in this world who are millionaires.

The real goal is a fulfilling venture that augments your income either a little or a lot. It all depends upon you and your idea. Think marriage. That's right, marriage. A good marriage is what you're after here whereby, in theory, you will stay with your concept for better or for worse. Some ideas are indeed big money ideas and some are not. It depends largely upon your dedication, imagination and your willingness to listen and learn at the early stages. Still you can't just aim for the biggest money-maker. Instead, you find the idea that's right for you and learn and grow with it, and then maybe your next idea will be the real bonanza. What's most essential is to get comfortable with the process.

The 'Sideswipe' Theory

In general, the best successes and greatest adventures do not belong to the rigid, but to those open to the new possibilities as they assume their direction. Be aware and prepared that opportunities may and will creep up or 'sideswipe' you as you assume one direction or another. Be ready to recognize and capitalize on these unexpected opportunities.

1) Refine Your Self-Understanding

Your first self-initiated venture is important because you learn so much about patience and perseverance, and hopefully you will not or have not spent yourself into a financial dream-killer situation. What follows are a series a exercises to help you explore and expand upon the three-stage idea-development process.

Connection #2
Who Are You? What Are You?

Scientist, blue-collar, white-collar, no collar, the exercise is still the same. Following is an connection exercise progression designed to help point you in the right direction. **Don't Rush.** This could take an evening or several weeks but do apportion your time so you will eventually finish. You are not allowed to give up halfway through.

The Present Me

1. When people ask what you do, you say, (list one primary occupation or whatever primarily occupies your weekday):

   "I am _____

   _____

   _____

   _____ "

2. List at least five things you love about what you do:

_____

_____

_____

_____

_____

3. List up to five things that you dislike about what you do:

_____

_____

_____

_____

_____

4. "People tell me that what they like most about me is:

_____

_____

_____

_____ "

5. "People are most bothered by the fact that I:

_____

_____

_____

_____ "

6. Aside from your primary occupation, list any other skills you have, whether proficient at them or not:

_____

_____

_____

_____

My Desires and Vision

7. "Aside from becoming more financially independent (we'll get to that), I would also like to be more:

_____

_____

_____

_____

_____ "

8. List at least three things that you'd like to see changed or improved in your community:

_____

_____

_____

9. List at least three things you'd like to see changed in the world:

_____

_____

_____

2) Determine Your Best Idea

The next exercise will help you to build on your self-understanding to determine your best idea.

Connection #3
Putting You and Your Vision into Action
(Finding your best idea)

1. List any ideas you've had in the past—any ideas for products or services, whether you acted upon them or not:

_____

_____

_____

_____

Remember to take all the time you need for the above. It is not a quiz and it's most definitely not a judgment on you. It's merely the most effective means we've discovered to help you find *your best starting point*; a sort of insurance policy to create maximum possibilities for your success. So relax. Have fun with it, because it will be the foundation from which you will build.

2. Delete, combine and add to your ideas from the list you generated in Step 1. Let your new self-understanding and your inner guidance lead you to the idea that is best for you at this point in your life. Write it down here for emphasis and focus.

I have completed the exercises in Connections 2 and 3 many times over the past eight years and have discovered an interesting pattern in my responses. No matter how many times I perform these exercises, I always find that the answers are relatively the same. This leads me to the following conclusion: regardless of how confused my conscious thoughts may be at times, my intuition knows what I should be doing and always brings me back to the same place. So, I've finally received the message, and I'm acting on it!

Another interesting phenomenon is that once I begin to realize the ideas which I am being drawn to, new space opens up in my life for additional ideas to surface over and above the initial venture.

What are the lessons that I can pass on to you?
- ❏ *Trust yourself.*
- ❏ *Act on the results of these exercises. It's the only way you can get past this point in your life.*
- ❏ *Be open to changes in the results of these exercises as your actions from previous exercises are realized.*

3) Be Open to New Ways of Thinking

Exploring new ideas and new paths always involves a little self-exploration and that can seem a little scary or just plain bothersome. Many of our clients find it easy, having been in some form of professional life for quite a while. Others aren't sure who they are or what they have, but interestingly enough, the second category is often the most creative because they haven't been excessively preconditioned or hardened by certain established or learned barriers. It is most helpful to remember that any life, any situation, can be observed in two ways: as overwhelming, hopeless, and depressing, or as chock full of possibilities, promise and adventure, no matter who you are and no matter what your current situation. Find the fun, find the adventure, or better said, *make* the fun, build the adventure. Any point can be a starting point upward.

Having said that, and hopefully having cleansed your idea-producing palate, you should now be ready for the most exciting aspect of your personal idea-profile and this part is quite a bit of fun because you'll not only create a lot of new possibilities, you'll learn new things about yourself.

Power-Up Tip #1
The Dream Ride

The title *dream ride* actually came from Bronson's personal and admittedly dangerous habit of coming up with his best ideas while driving or riding his mountain-bike. There they'd hit him and he'd frantically scribble them down before he really hit someone else. Obviously, we would never endorse writing while driving unless you're lucky enough to have a dictaphone or tape recorder or a gracious passenger who will write for you.

But for us, it was all that daydreaming and driving that really got our creative juices flowing: new places = new ideas. The essence of the dream ride exercise for most of you involves simply carrying around a little pen and pocket notebook with you wherever you go. Whenever you have a thought, even a scant notion or question about something, enter it in your notebook.

As you occasionally refer back to your responses in the initial part of this exercise (some of which you may add to as time goes by), make notes about any ideas that might suit you; what do you like?

What could you make or what service could you create? Remember that money is not an issue yet. First, let's make sure you're matched up with the best idea and then we'll deal with the other issues in later chapters. Aside from money, which most of us would like to have more of, what else makes you happy, and would you do more of it if you could make money at it? Write it all down.

What do you do that makes you happy that you wish you had more time to do? What talents do you have or could you develop to enable you to live that dream? Do you want your hobby to grow until it eventually becomes a vocation?

Naturally, we've seen quite a few of these notebooks from people who previously thought they couldn't fill one page. And of course, we have piles of our own. Loads of our own ideas and especially loads of *fragments*. And it's those fragments, those puzzle-pieces, that are most valuable.

Take several days, weeks or even a couple of months note-writing (these could be some of the most important decisions of your life, so take whatever time you need). Anxious people rush to failure, but enthusiastic people step to success.

And test, test, test! Tests make or break. Tests preserve or insure your dreams. So find ways to test your idea(s) even from the most scant beginnings—like when we're dream riding—exploring new ideas as we explore our own identities. As we suggested earlier, it's scary stuff, looking at what we are and what we're not; until we remember that the very purpose of this entire chapter is simply to create a platform, a jumping-off point not from what we are or are not, but *where we wanna be*.

Along with a new idea, this is about creating a new you, a new success or even a first success. As you undertake this process, you'll discover that no matter who you are or how successful or unsuccessful you have been, you have learned something every day. Maybe you haven't learned how to *apply* or incorporate all those daily issues you've had, and that's why this initial chapter is so important.

Want a better life? We don't have the answer—no TV commercial has the answer, no matchbook cover has the answer, and no parent or relative has the answer. They're all just puzzle-pieces—opinions. It's *you* who must make the final decision as to what might be the most fulfilling and challenging for you. All throughout the process of developing and nurturing your ideas, you may occasionally find yourself temporarily short of certain resources, but you'll always have an abundance of opinions which you must either validate or discard.

"But It's a Secret!"

Does fear kill or preserve an idea? What do you need to protect an idea to ensure its success? If you talk about it with your friends, are they going to steal it? We know that this is a great concern to a vast majority of our readers and clientele, and we address the issue at various points in our progress.

Remember that ideas, no matter how spectacular, are only the beginning. In fact, free, competitive markets always consist of similar competitive products. Even if two ideas appeared to be almost identical, they could each still legitimately earn a share of the market. Further, no two concepts, even if identical, ever hit the market in the same way.

But in order to ensure that you don't restrict your creativity and potential with fear, we suggest that you think in terms of *degrees*. If you are a certified welder, or maybe you have a Ph D. in Psychology, or perhaps you're an experienced home builder, the attendant certifications that accompany these competencies are ones you and you alone have earned. If someone stole the degree that belonged to you, all they'd have is the paper certification without the vital substance. To really get your concept, they'd have to steal your brain too!

So for most readers, part of your best protection is that your concept is too much a part of you for someone to come along and take it. Then there's the issue of momentum. Hopefully, you'll use this book to be the most intelligent and aggressive in your marketplace which is, in our opinion, your best protection, i.e. earning a comfortable market share that's yours and yours alone.

Then there are the various patent, copyright, and trademark issues which we will go over in Chapter 4. These issues will show you that the law is on the side of the dedicated originator. So protect, register, copyright, trademark, and patent pend by all means. Just be frugal, and don't let paranoia kill the potential development of a good idea. You have to trust some people, and ultimately you will find those people. *And be aggressive in your marketplace.*

The world is full of great beginning ideas that are totally worthless only because nobody knew or connected with those who might have known how to act upon them. So explore on, dream on, and dream without fear.

At this point, you will have reached one of two stages: you either have a lot of puzzle-pieces in the form of notes, or have added more dimension to an idea you already had, i.e. you are more certain about how to better direct that idea. In either case, it is now time to throw those notes on a table and see what puzzle-pieces fit. What fragments have you come up with that will constitute the best idea for you to pursue? Do not focus at this point on the money or labor you think it's going to take to develop your idea. What's crucial now is the proper starting point.

When you have compiled your notes, or when you are fairly certain you know the direction in which you want to head, lay all your stuff (notes, etc.) on a table somewhere and begin putting the pieces together. Take heart—the answers shouldn't hit you right away. This is an intake time. You're a detective. We are working up to the point where you will learn how to relate your ideas with the appropriate potential contacts.

Summary

This is the point where dream becomes child, takes on a heartbeat and some tangibility. This chapter is crucial for helping to map out a clearer definition of your idea. To do this, you must be open to possibilities you had not previously considered.

1) Refine Your Self-Understanding

❏ Complete Connection #2

2) Determine Your Best Idea

❏ Complete Connection #3
❏ Be sure you've settled upon the best idea. Be certain that it's really a part of your personality.
❏ Do you really like your idea?
❏ Is this something that's so much a part of you that you'll stay married to it for better or for worse?
❏ Will you be flexible as market reaction dictates turns and changes not previously planned for or expected?
❏ Does your concept possess 'evergreen potential,' i.e. perpetuity in the marketplace?

❏ Can it be utilized, improved, redeveloped and made available year after year, like a hammer in a hardware store? Unless you're developing a fad-production business, stay away from fads unless you have a program for delivering follow-up products. The money-making pet rock and wall-walker were exceptions, not rules.
❏ Study the feedback until you really understand the best means for your concept.

3) Be Open to New Ways of Thinking

❏ Take a Dream Ride—Tip #1.
❏ Show flexibility.
  ❏ Listen intently to the feedback and new understandings you have gained about both yourself and your idea.
  ❏ Be open to 'sideswipes'—directions not previously anticipated.
❏ Continue to make notes of your random and fragmented thoughts.
  ❏ Carry a little notebook. 📖
  ❏ Write it down! ✍
❏ Once again, dump your ideas on the kitchen table and look for patterns in your thinking.
❏ Keep at it!

Potential Challenges and Solutions

Challenge: Can't find an idea.

Solution: Fear of failure for those who have tried and failed before is understandable, but then again, you never had this book to help you before either. Fear of failure from those who have never tried a venture before is less understandable. First of all, you know some failures are unavoidable components of eventual success. Secondly, how are you going to know what you've got unless you give it a try?

Since we've attempted to take most of the financial risk out of it, the worst that can happen is that you will enhance your education about something and thus increase your value as a human being.

Assert your right to become a full and fulfilled soul. Don't be shy. Hitting upon the wrong idea generally results from bad listening or unrealistic planning. If you're building a boat, you don't begin by building a QE2.

Work and grow within your gifts and abilities. Even something new must have a characteristic that somehow reflects that which has always been a part of you.

Challenge: Impatience/Anxiousness.

Solution: Enthusiasm will give your idea energy, anxiousness will rush you to the wrong decision. Take your time and be open to the possibility that you may have not yet settled upon the best idea for you.

Challenge: Excessive focus on financial gain.

Solution: This book is designed to help you make more money. But orient first on your personal interests, then the appropriate financial formulas will follow.

Before You Continue...

- ❏ Can you describe your idea clearly and concisely?
- ❏ Is there a market for your idea?
- ❏ If so, where is it and what percentage of the overall population is it?
- ❏ What might your retail price be?
- ❏ What do other people think? (via Reaction Forms in upcoming chapters.)
- ❏ Do you have or can you develop any talent relative to any phase of the development of this idea?
- ❏ Are you a resource or a liability to your own idea?
- ❏ Is your idea useful, entertaining, etc? In other words, which of the following human needs and emotions does it appeal to, as pertaining to both your own needs and those of your potential customers:
  - ❏ Love, greater feeling of self-worth
  - ❏ Recognition/acknowledgement/popularity/pride
  - ❏ Success/personal achievement
  - ❏ Self-congratulation/ego-gratification
  - ❏ Physical comfort and/or improvement, pleasure
  - ❏ Reduced fear (security)—emotional/financial
  - ❏ Creativity enhancement/skill development
  - ❏ Physical attractiveness
  - ❏ Heightened convenience/independence

Chapter Three

Assessment
The Best Ways to Test Your Idea

> *"Life is either a daring adventure or it is nothing."*
> **Helen Keller**

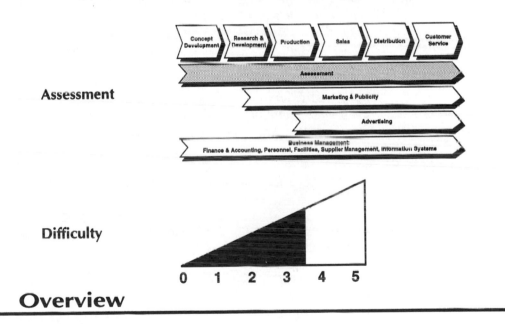

Assessment

Difficulty

0 1 2 3 4 5

Overview

It's not enough to have an idea, even a great idea. It's having the persistence and vision to find out how you need to mix with the world in order to turn that concept into something profitable. This chapter will help you to begin those vital evaluation steps.

Assessment

Action Steps

1) Develop a familiarity and comfort with your idea.
2) Systematically seek out a broad range of opinions.
3) Analyze initial responses.

Alfred Hitchcock. The name immediately evokes an entire concept. His genius of suspense, his almost extrasensory ability to thrill and delight you.

Bronson

In August of 1976, I had the good fortune of meeting him. It was late at night of course. We were both vacationing at the Mauna Kea resort in Hawaii. I walked into the seaside bar for a late night drink and there he was—alone, solemn, yet somehow approachable.

It was a Hawaiian-style, open air bar with rustling tropical plants wiggling their leaves, like a thousand dancing fingers. A mysterious darkness seemed to prevail, with most of the illumination coming from the little enclosed table candles. One of these candles cast an eerie glow under Mr. Hitchcock's face.

I had every reason to turn and run. The sense of danger, the awesomeness of a celebrity. What could a young fan like me say to such a complete master who actually seemed to control the environment! I asked him if he wanted some company and he said,"Yes!" (Does it pay to take a chance or what!)

I can still recite that twenty-minute conversation word-for-word and describe every nuance. I was a young writer and had yet to discover the focus of my talent.

During one segment of that conversation, I asked him outright what advice he could give a young upstart writer who wanted to be commercially successful.

"My dear boy," he slowly turned toward me as he spoke, that underlighting now giving him a other-than-human appearance. In that great warm and authoritative soft British bellow, he continued, "You've got to know what your audience is theeenking."

Know what your audience is thinking—my first lesson in the development of a major selling point of my career. What do they want out there, and how can I give it to them?

Learning to develop good ideas has been a specialty of mine. Why do some grow and others die? Interestingly enough, Hitchcock helped take the mystery out of it for me. Now I know how to do my homework.

1) Develop a Familiarity and Comfort with Your Idea

So here you are. You think you're all ready to forge ahead and see if your idea will hold water. Do you really have a good idea? We're going to be a little harsh on you for a a bit to help reduce your chances of expending your energies in the wrong direction, and should the idea hold water, guide you every way we can in the right direction.

If we send you back to the first chapter, it's only to increase your chances of success. If you don't agree with us, that's your right. Answer the following questions honestly:

Is your idea something you just thought of the other day? You may have said to yourself, "Yeah, that's as good an idea as any." Does this describe you at all? That's fine. Go back to Chapter 1 and start over.

Are you ready to risk a chunk of your hard-earned money on your idea? You are? Okay, you're demoted. You may be too anxious to see your idea clearly. Go back and make sure you've thought it through. Take the time to give your inspirations a healthy birth.

Are you afraid of failure? Are you worried that your idea may not work out and that you'll be wasting your time? Let us tell you. We sure are. We want everything we do to lead to success. Note that we use the word 'lead.' Failures are nothing more than temporary detours on your path to success. They are just one crucial component of the success formula. Wear your faults like a badge. If you understand what went wrong and how to make it right, you'll continually be able to promote your cause.

All businesses are in business to solve a particular problem. They attempt to turn that problem into an opportunity and hence, profit. See how important your failures can be?

So, you're confident enough about your idea to have continued on. What would a major advertising agency or marketing company do at this point? If they liked the idea, they might spend thousands of dollars, at the very least, to test the concept, then design, develop, promote and get it out to market.

Many concepts die very expensive deaths, not always because they are bad products. The successful development of a product or service depends on the creative and technical abilities or limitations of that particular developer.

Bad planning, bad feedback, and most importantly, bad listening wastes money. Bad listening destroys spaceships and melts nuclear reactors. We must do our share to avoid that, whether we are developing a product for a company or ourselves.

In the late 80's, I was a space shuttle flight controller at Mission Control in  *Houston. I was involved in many re-engineering teams after the Challenger accident to help re-think Mission Control's operational processes. As you can imagine, the focus on safety was paramount in this post-Challenger era, and NASA instituted a new, anonymous safety reporting system. However, even in this heightened awareness environment, people were acting according to human nature by regularly trying to save face.*

On one particular team in which I was involved, an issue arose concerning how software commands would be sent to the space shuttle when it was in orbit. I knew the proposed method was unsafe and presented my position to the group. I was told repeatedly by the team leader that I was incorrect. I believe I was getting this response because it would have taken TOO MUCH TIME to check out my theory.

Not being one for bureaucracy, and thinking the problem was only going to get worse if something wasn't done immediately, I bypassed the safety reporting system and went directly to the program director. He was very open to what I had to say, and within a week, the problem was resolved.

The lesson here is to pay attention to what people are telling you and take the time to check out their input. It's important to remember that even new technologies and enhanced safety systems are still operated by people.

First of all, aside from yourself, determine who your idea will benefit. If you think it's only the user, think again. What about the distributors, manufacturers, all of the people involved in the production of the item before it reaches its final destination?

Basic Protection

Before we get into our preliminary testing phase, there are many readers who are afraid that someone out there may just steal their idea. Most of the time, you'll find that people are trustworthy, but to put your mind at ease, you could do the following: Write down a brief description of your concept, including any supporting documentation. Make two copies and mail one to your lawyer and one to yourself. They are to be kept sealed until needed.

If your idea is sufficiently unique, have your attorney (or find an attorney) begin the patent process. Additionally, if you are exploring your idea with a potential manufacturer, you can ask him to sign a statement that he will not replicate the idea you are about to discuss. It's also prudent to maintain a log, dating and documenting your progress.

Whatever you do, if you insist on being paranoid, don't use it as an excuse to interfere with your progress. After all, you're going to become so knowledgeable about your concept, you'll be the authority.

When we come up with a new marketing scheme or product, we're generally flattered and amused by our imitators. Flattered because they copied our idea, and amused because they can rarely do it as well or as cost-effectively as we can.

In short, people are desperate for good ideas because they haven't learned to develop their own creative process by following our guidelines. They are afraid of the idea of the creative process. These types of people generally don't have what it takes to make an idea happen because they are not really a part of its birth. Thieves always get caught, either by others or themselves.

But all philosophy aside, remember that in business ventures there is only one definition of a gift. A gift is any work, money, anything you contribute without a written agreement in advance. Always find a way to move ahead, but don't ever downplay the need to protect yourself.

So, if you're putting together a product, make sure that exact product is not already on the market. As long as you make an improvement or some significant modification, then you should be able to get your patent, if necessary, and move forward.

Millions of you have service or product ideas that may not require a patent. For the particular state you're living in, an attorney would best advise you in all areas of product protection.

It will take a lot more homework before your idea is actually ready for the development stages. You don't know exactly what you've got yet. Over and over again, we will remind you to keep thinking results— don't get stuck.

2) Systematically Seek Out a Broad Range of Opinions

One fall, I decided to enter an international business plan competition to see how my business and marketing ideas could stand up to international cast of competitors. I joined ranks with a great friend of mine, and we locked ourselves away for several weeks to develop a complete business plan for a video teleconferencing services business.

After we were sick of being stuck in a stuffy room together, we thought it would be a good idea to invite all of the business acquaintances we could think of to a trial presentation of our business plan. These people were lawyers, accountants, venture capitalists, consultants, and business owners. To our great surprise, most of them actually attended our presentation. We didn't offer them anything for their time, not even refreshments, just a please and a thank you.

After we had concluded our presentation, they grilled us with questions for almost an hour, and we had plenty of our own questions for them. The next week, we incorporated every single good idea. It improved our plan tremendously, and we were called a month later with an invitation to compete in the oral portion of the contest with four other contestants from a pool over 200 entries from around the world.

We didn't win in the end (although we did have the best plan), but we learned the value of input from our business acquaintances. I believe that we would not have made it to the oral portion of the competition without their valued, but FREE advice.

Time to pick some brains. There are scores of people out there who will be only too glad to give you free time and advice—FREE ADVICE. Some of it will be questionable, but some of it will prove highly valuable. As you become more intimate with your product, and if you use this book as a guide, you'll soon learn to decipher the usable from the stuff you throw away.

We said free advice. Why will so many experts generally be glad to give you some free time? If your product takes off, some of these people know they may become involved in the production process. A little investment of their time could really pay off.

Tell these valued advisors what you are thinking of and make notes. You're not always going to like what you hear but a little criticism can save you a fortune. Remember that underwater safety switch we described in the last chapter? Here's a good lesson: *After* we gave the distributors thousands of these single switches, we met with them to find out how it was doing. Unanimously, they told us there was no market for a single switch, only a *double* switch. Had we picked their brains before we hit the drawing board, the client would have saved a lot of time and money.

Senior Helpers

Pick brains FIRST. Talk to authorities. Don't assume you know it all just because you were successful in another career. A number of our clients are in their sixties and seventies and are wealthy. Almost invariably, the first thing we work to convey to them is just because they turned sixty and were successful at one thing, doesn't automatically make them an authority on everything.

However, in no way will I ever deny that one of your greatest potential assets for procedural guidance could be the great and untapped wealth of retired persons and senior citizens. Seek them out via your local senior citizens organizations. Generally, you'll make some great friends and your product will enjoy a much better end result to success. Seek out the Service Core of Retired Executives.

Very often, I tap into my consortium of seniors when I am undertaking a new venture. When I used to live in Los Angeles, I had a next-door neighbor named Howard Miller. I can tell you that he didn't reach his nineties by being anybody's fool. What a privileged life I had to have had so much wisdom right next door.

Wisdom is knowledge of what is true or correct coupled with good judgment. It's the ultimate reward for all your triumphs and your screw-ups. In fact, I've learned much more from the mistakes of others, than even from my own cache of faux pas.

Keep the following in mind: As long as your idea has some merit to someone, there's always a way to put it together. Listen, think and accept no one as final authority except yourself.

We actually know someone who spent almost $150,000 to make a mold for the mass production of his product in plastic. Any injection-molder will tell you that he could make a similar mold for only a few hundred dollars.

We've discussed basic products so our points would be clearly understood, but many readers have very complex ideas or services. Essentially, the same query-approaches apply. In fact, if your idea is service-oriented, you can often see the possibilities blossoming at a very rapid rate.

Let's suppose you want to create an information source for a senior citizens organization. You might begin by discussing it with a local senior center, or even city hall. Such was the case in New Bedford, Massachusetts. A house-wife, whose children had grown and left the nest, wound up successfully getting start-up funds and now runs a newspaper exclusively for seniors.

She had done some writing in the past and she wanted to make a use-ful contribution to her community. Her paper is now a model for simi-lar efforts around the country. All she began with was an intelligent idea that complimented her potential, and a little homework. What a perfect inspiration and example of finding one's star.

Some people may call some of our research tactics a form of networking. It's actually a form of reverse consulting. Networking implies talking business at parties. We don't like that. For now, when you're at a party, have fun. Go easy on your friends. You want customer reaction but spread your inquiries around or you'll be the death of any party.

Take Hitchcock's advice. Talk to potential customers. What do they want from a better widget? And what about the existing product that may be similar to yours? What's wrong with it and why is yours an improvement over it? What are the problems that you can eliminate? Ask, Explore, LISTEN and Digest. Keep thinking: Concept, Research, Refine the Concept, Focus the Research.

As you progress in this area, something exciting begins to happen. Your ideas begin to come into focus. As the dust settles, you have begun to get a much better idea of where you're going and how to get there. Best of all, you haven't spent thousands of dollars to test your market or shape your gem. For this chapter, you have spent some money on gas, phone calls and some more pads and pencils. That's a reasonable invest-ment to explore your dream.

How's your concept building? Are you ready to make it come to life? Let's find out.

The Expensive Evaluation that Costs You Nothing

Qualified field experts and most companies with start-up products often spend more on evaluating the feasibility of a product/service than most of us might see in our lifetimes. But then why are so many millions of everyday people like you successfully launching concepts with hard-ly any resources? The reason is simple; because you *can* get vital and often valuable feedback on your prototypes, plans, etc. *without* all the expense and often with hardly *any* of the expense.

The people you shall seek feedback from are broken down into three cat-egories: personal friends, professional people that you know, and finally, people that you *don't* know who have some relevance to your venture with respect to production, prototype planning and overall marketing. Remember, you are not to hire anyone at this point. If you do, you might financially discourage yourself in a hurry. What we're really doing is making sure that our next step will be our most sensible one.

Here Comes that Old Paranoia

You're still concerned about the protection of your idea and in this new edition, we delve into most of the protection issues far more aggressively. You may want to go through Chapter 4 right now and then come back and finish the rest of this chapter. Our own view is that while theft can occur, and while some ventures require patent attorneys, for the most part in today's marketplace, your best protection is your personal commitment to your own special venture. Don't be afraid to learn and then to aggressively apply what you have learned to your sales efforts.

As we write and research, we have gone back to several patent attorneys and scores of associates and our stories are all the same; most people you deal with who are in the various facets of legitimate business are trustworthy and they would have to be or *nobody* would deal with them. While always respecting the privacy of our clientele, we have (with permission) talked about or pitched thousands of ideas with potential contacts and no one has ever stolen an idea from us. Most of our associates share this feeling.

Then we'll be giving an interview or seminar and someone will tell us that they had an idea for a better rake or book or you-name-it. "Next thing I know," they'd tell us, "someone else is coming out with *my* idea." 99% of the time, this happens because either someone did indeed come up with a similar idea all on their own and this happens. Sometimes people observe similar trends and resultant needs based upon these trends and hence come up with similar ideas, like the computer, the fax machine or the chocolate-chip cookie, again, you-name-it! Well, that's just free enterprise.

Don't *ever* aim for or expect 100% of any market. That's unrealistic. What is realistic is that you create, listen, learn, bend, adjust, and thrive and survive by *earning* your *marketshare*, your piece of the pie.

Going back to the patent attorneys we have interviewed, most expressed concern that so many clients would spend so much money on protection and then fail because they spent no energy on *marketing*. When *Good Idea! Now What?* was first written, one attorney jokingly suggested it be called, *Good Idea! So What!* But looking back, his idea wasn't all that unrealistic because his title made it clear; anyone can have a good idea. It's the ability to act upon that idea and respond effectively to the needs of the correct market that will make it successful.

And if you still have concerns when speaking to certain parties, describe your idea in general terms. Often an idea can be conveyed without giving away details, allowing the potential consultant to understand the prospective market, and to give opinions.

Ultimately, whatever protection you may or may not have, in order to connect and move ahead you have to trust some people. So yes, be careful; don't give away the farm, don't spend a lot of money to start the idea, but on the other side, don't use paranoia as an excuse for not progressing. In our opinion, your commitment to finding the right marketplace is your best protection and your best chance at success. So assuming now that you may have already read Chapter 4 if you were so inclined, let's now proceed with this vital evaluation phase.

3) Analyze Initial Responses

Connection #4
The Reaction Formulation

The purpose of this connection exercise is to determine how best your idea suits you. We are not simply talking about need or marketability. What we are most interested in here is finding out how well your idea will fit you. Assuming your concept has survived our previous interrogatories, let us now try to get an indication of what the rest of the world thinks. Now of course the ultimate test is whether the end user (customer) buys (accepts) it, but this next evaluation is a strong one.

Following is the initial primary reaction category. Under each heading, get opinions from each group and evaluate and summarize their reactions as briefly as possible.

- Do they like it? If so or no, why?
- What changes would they make?
- What retail price would they pay for it?
- What manufacturing procedure might they follow?
- Who or where do they think the customers are?
- How would they propose reaching the customers?
- Why do you think they reacted the way they did?
- Who do they know that might be able to assist you?

Category 1 - Personal (friends, relatives, co-workers)

Name   **Opinion**

_____

_____

_____

Your Reaction   _____

_____

_____

_____

Name   **Opinion**

_____

_____

_____

Your Reaction   _____

_____

_____

_____

Name   **Opinion**

_____

_____

_____

Your Reaction   _____

_____

_____

_____

Category 2 - Professional Acquaintances

Name   **Opinion**

_____

_____

_____

Your Reaction   _____

_____

_____

_____

Name   **Opinion**

_____

_____

_____

Your Reaction   _____

_____

_____

_____

Name   **Opinion**

_____

_____

_____

Your Reaction   _____

_____

_____

_____

Category 3 - Other Relevant People

Name   **Opinion**

_____

_____

_____

Your Reaction   _____

_____

_____

_____

Name   **Opinion**

_____

_____

_____

Your Reaction   _____

_____

_____

_____

Name   **Opinion**

_____

_____

_____

Your Reaction   _____

_____

_____

_____

Assessment

Note: In filling out these forms, be sure to list subject's possible relevancy to your concept! You may make additional copies of any of the forms in this book for your own personal use.

Briefly summarize all of the opinions:

_____

_____

_____

_____

_____

Your Idea Reference Page

You've spent a long time getting to this point and you've sought out many preliminary evaluations. Hopefully, you've done a $100,000 job for either very little or no money at all.

Before completing this page, study your progress. How has your idea evolved? How much money and time have you saved by utilizing this chapter? How good of a listener have you been? Do you now have a better focus on your market (who will really buy what you're selling, and who won't)?

Having studied the new puzzle pieces in this chapter, now describe your concept and the changes:

My New and Better Idea Is:

_____

_____

_____

_____

_____

Parties and Barflies

Earlier on we admonished you not to bore people at parties. Well now you have something more interesting. If you feel sufficiently comfortable about your concept, test it, at least verbally and maybe just in general terms, at parties or see how it flies at the local bar, etc.—any gathering where people feel relaxed and where you'll hear what you need to hear instead of what you want to hear.

Summary

This is the point where the dream assumes sufficient shape to relate it to other people. A dreamer who wants really wants dreams to happen will listen carefully and patiently. Don't fight with your critics; seek them out and draw them out. The better you've done with these three prior chapters, the fewer regrets you'll encounter in the future. Your idea should be much improved, but still, it is only as good as your ability to earn your market share. Make sure that you:

1) Develop a Familiarity and Comfort With Your Idea

❏ Secure appropriate protection for your idea. Protect but don't let fear of theft prevent your progress. For additional information on protection issues, see Chapter 4.

2) Systematically Seek Out a Broad Range of Opinions

❏ Seek out consultations from authorities at every level.
1) Personal—friends, relatives, and co-workers
2) Professional acquaintances
3) Other relevant people
❏ Listen carefully, without ego.
❏ Ask the valuable authorities every question you can think up concerning your project.

3) Analyze Initial Responses

❏ Complete Connection #4.
❏ Incorporate the feedback to make a better product.

Potential Challenges and Solutions

Challenge: Insecure about releasing the idea without sufficient patent protection.

Solution: People generally have the following choices once they have received their patents: They can sell or lease the idea, they can put the patent certificate on a shelf to show their grandchildren, or they can make the venture happen themselves.

Though many of you do require exacting protection, review all the alternatives with your attorney. Get your protection and then move ahead. In my experience, I have seen paranoia kill more ideas than even greed kills.

Your other innate protection is that, for most cases, no one has your specific technical skills to make your venture successful. This book has shown you that you have things of far greater value to offer your prospects, i.e. your know-how from concept all the way to customer.

Challenge: Can't find authorities to talk to.

Solution: For simple products or ideas, it's just a matter of time before you track down the right people. The only problem may be distance.

If you live too far away from the right people, don't just send your product with a letter. Before you run up huge phone bills, see if your target company has a toll-free phone number. Your local library should have a copy of AT&T's 1-800 directory, and sometimes it is available on CD ROM.

If your venture is fairly sophisticated, break it down into components and seek out the makers of those individual components.

You can also locate products with some similarities to yours which might be marketed in a fashion similar to yours. Those experts could also benefit from your marketing prowess.

Challenge: Afraid or unable to approach these experts.

Solution: People are people first, just like you. Many of this country's biggest success stories were once nothing but an idea, maybe like yours. Those types often welcome someone with a similar ambition.

If someone refuses to meet with you, after much effort on your part, move on. After you've succeeded, let them come crawling to you.

If someone acts in a very intimidating manner towards you, don't be affected by it. You are there for knowledge. If you have to cut the meeting short, leave politely and seek your information elsewhere. There are plenty of successful human beings out there who can help you and who will treat you with respect.

Before You Continue...

❑ Have you found an adequate means to relate, test, or demonstrate your idea? There's always some way to relate it, even in the most general terms.

❑ Remember that enterprises are all ultimately dependent upon the support of the appropriate people. Are you seeking them out?

Chapter Four

Do It Yourself R&D
Creating a Model and Protecting It

> *"If you don't think of the future, you cannot have one."*
>
> **Anonymous**

Research and Development

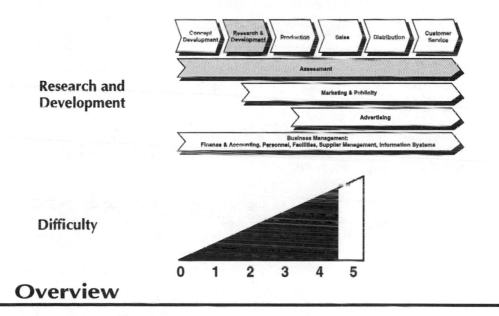

Difficulty

0   1   2   3   4   5

Overview

It doesn't necessarily take money to make money. What it does require are the right resources, right team and perhaps a corner of the living room, kitchen, garage or basement.

Action Steps

1) Bring the idea into a tangible form.
2) Implement low-cost ways to utilize effective resources.
3) Pursue protection if necessary.

1) Bring the Idea into a Tangible Form

Science fiction films have become so creative and convincing, that we essentially accept their portrayals of the future as gospel. Deep space adventures are presented with a clever intermesh of intelligence, compassion and photon torpedoes. We often find ourselves focusing on the melodrama, accepting all the glitzy special effects as standard background.

No space vehicle or home will be complete without a transporter which will demolecularize any human or object and make it come to life at any other given point in the universe.

If you think transporters are either totally fictitious or light years away, with no bearing on today's world, think again. Star Trek has landed at places like the GE Plastics Technology Division in Pittsfield, Massachusetts.

Things of all types, born of ideas, are transformed from the center of the mind onto a computer screen, where it may be plainly seen from all perspectives. It does not stop there.

Right there, within the heart of the computer, the image can be engineered, even to the point of stress analysis and performance testing. Turn on the transporter. Here comes the real magic. Before thousands of dollars have been spent drafting, testing, etc., the computer actually transforms the design into a physical product mold, from which the product can be made. Computer aided design and engineering is carried out at many levels in many companies throughout the world. These are the ultimate dream-into-reality machines, riding on the leading edge of the future. They are virtually concept to customer at the push of a button, but they cannot tell us if the people will actually accept a product no matter how perfect it may be.

We operate from the standpoint that most readers do not yet have access to such million-dollar technology, but we shall still achieve viable test results well within or below your budget. You're about to discover the vast difference between image and substance. The development process is also the second phase of the evaluation process. Here is where we beam our ideas into something real. You've kicked your idea around with everyone. Some of your friends will think you're really into something interesting. Some think you're all talk. Attitudes will really change as your image transforms into substance; as your dedication gives steam and energy to what began simply in your head and heart. How do you build a model if you've never built one before? Do you begin at the beginning? Not necessarily. But you must begin.

In college I took a few art courses. Though I contend it was to escape from the  *pressures of my other studies, my poor art teachers will insist that I did it to prove that I was the world's worst artist.*

I couldn't paint. I couldn't sculpt. I just never knew how to get a piece going. Finally, an artist got a hold of me. She gave me a brush, paints and a blank canvas and said, "Just throw something, anything on the canvas and don't think about it."

I did this for several sessions. I never became a very good artist. It's just not a gift of mine. I did continue to improve a little. The vital point is to let your models evolve no matter how sketchy or sloppy the beginning is. Remember the very adult message from Peter Pan: "If you don't dream, how will your dreams come true?"

Create Initial Model

Don't get so confused or rigid that you're afraid to begin. Now that your ideas are starting to come into focus, throw it on the canvas or paper or whatever. You probably won't love what you see at first. Doing is more important than asking why at this stage.

Even if the physical birth of your idea is a little ugly, don't worry about it. At least it's a birth. The first three chapters have already helped you build a wealth of knowledge. Don't be too disappointed at this stage. This is a time to be flexible.

Too many times in our careers we have seen great ideas get trashed just as soon as their creators decide an obstacle is too great to overcome. This sense of overwhelm is common. The advantage you have now with this book is that you can press on, bit by bit, if necessary, without draining your bank account.

I have a buddy in Vermont named Skip Morrow. He was always subjecting us to nutty ideas and wacky illustrations. We all knew he was going someplace, but we didn't know when he would actually be admitted.

Finally, he assembled some of his illustrations to create a comic calendar about cats. Though I thought the sketches were kind of cute, I didn't see how all this wackiness could translate into any kind of unique earnings.

A few years passed when, in a bookstore one day, I saw it: "The Official 'I Hate Cats' Book," written and illustrated by none other than Skip Morrow. Skip went on to enjoy many bestsellers and now creates a successful line of greeting cards, as well as a thousand other ideas.

He knew his talent, developed it and got it on paper. This creative genius took his rebellious, unconventional thoughts and stayed with them. Now, instead of living in an institution, he has become one. Excited, alive and ever driven by his creativity—from tenacious concept to customer. May we all reach that level one day.

2) Implement Low-Cost Ways to Utilize Effective Resources

If you don't try to make your idea happen, it will most likely never become real. Your aim here is to create something that will help start the wheels of production turning. Don't cut corners. You could imagine that you could go to a particular manufacturer and tell him about, and maybe sell him, your concept. Most major manufacturers get these kinds of proposals every day from starry-eyed conceptualists.

Our experience has taught us that this is not the best way to make your product come to life. As we mentioned earlier, consult with the heavies, but assemble the overall technology yourself. The working or nearly-working model is of much greater financial benefit to you than just an idea.

You worked hard to get that idea! Are you just going to give it away for a few dollars when you can make it yourself? But what if you could turn many of these sizable corporate heavies into valuable consultants for your enterprise and still own your project? Read on.

There is a barrier here, and it's generally you. If asked to come up with the key point that separates the successes from the failures at this stage, we arrive at one simple stumbling point: shyness. Too many people are afraid of looking foolish and will therefore not take the appropriate chances of making low-level presentations which, in turn, can lead to greater-level presentations. It's important to bear in mind that this is the time to make mistakes. This is the time to learn, and you are making these initial presentations to learn.

We get letters daily, almost always containing these phrases; "I'm no mechanic. I'm no artist. I'm no sculptor. I'm afraid to approach person 'X'. I'm no writer." In order to save a host of stamps, allow us to respond collectively. We're not interested in what you can't do. We're only interested in working with what you've got. Just talk to these people as people, discover what you have in common and learn, learn, learn!

If your idea is a physical product, make it—out of clay, popsicle sticks, wires, or whatever. Have fun. Relive your childhood. Creativity is fun because you're giving birth to something new that has never been done quite like you're doing it.

Once you feel you have a rough idea of what you wish your blob of clay would have looked like, take your blob to your local starving artist or sculptor or drafting student. Tell them what you were trying to do, get a solid price (anywhere from free to $100, or find someone else) and a firm deadline (one-to-four weeks depending on the sophistication of your blob).

Warn your model-refiner that you may call once or twice with a few slight modifications. It's important to be clear about your thoughts, and it's equally important for the artist to be sufficiently flexible in order make your idea happen. Establish a clear rapport from the beginning.

If your project requires drawings, diagrams, or a proposal, do what you can first, and then follow the above procedures. Written descriptions can be a bit more traumatic for many, but they shouldn't be. As you write, pretend you're writing a letter to your best friend or anyone else who you feel can understand what your thoughts mean. If you still have a problem, get a little tape-recorder and talk away, or work it out on your personal computer if you have one.

If your written proposal doesn't convey what it should to your particular target, bring it to your local high school English teacher who may be willing to refine your draft for free or for a modest fee (same formula as with models described earlier). Just remember there's always a way to do it and do it well. Don't look for excuses for yourself. That's the easy way to quit.

A few weeks later, you'll see the first signs of genuine encouragement for your project. That star we've been looking for and struggling with from page one suddenly is showing some promise of life—from brain and heart to something real and potentially commercially viable.

When you get the preliminary phase product in your hands, hold it, stare at it, sleep with it, make notes about it. Get it into your psychological bloodstream. You can see how you're increasing the value of your idea for yourself. Aren't you glad you didn't run to the first major manufacturer you could find? We're still in two phases simultaneously—development and assessment. As things develop, you evaluate, assess and make the appropriate modifications that permit you to move forward. Let's really get a jump on those manufacturers. Let's make a working model. It doesn't matter at this point how well it works, as long as it works. It merely has to make a point that it can do what you promise.

Look what you've done. You don't need an expert to tell you that it's not perfect, but is it something real that begins to validate your dreams? At this point, many of you are so excited that you're ready to go running to the nearest manufacturer or distributor or franchise attorney for instant wealth, fame or whatever. You've made it this far, now all you want to do is get it out on the market.

Most of you, however, are not ready yet to go to market. So if you begin to work with a manufacturer at this level of unreadiness, what happens to your own credibility, value and momentum? If your idea is more in the service realm, all down on paper and ready to wow your prospects, stop!

We interrupt this chapter for an important debriefing...

3) Pursue Protection if Necessary

Soon you will be scheduling a meeting with a group of potential producers of your idea. Before you meet with them, you will want to have some working knowledge of product protection. So, we've interrupted Chapter 4 to address many of your questions and concerns about concept protection. Personally, we simply keep a written track record and dated journal of all our concepts. Yet in hundreds of radio interviews, almost a third of the callers are totally focused and concerned about theft and protection. How can they be sure their concept won't be stolen? The following is a reflection of almost three decades of concept development and why we personally believe that while patents may be crucial for some concepts, momentum certainly is critical for the success.

Power-Up Tip #2
Patents, Protection, Paranoia,
Copyrights & Trademarks

"Yeah, I've got a good idea, alright. In fact, I bet it's so good, that's some-one's going to steal it if I talk to anyone about it. I've heard stories. But I have to relate this to some people or companies. What should I do? Must I have a patent at this stage? What if my idea doesn't make millions? Are there less expensive alternatives?"

This is the vital section, the one that even many experts just won't touch. Many recent articles about idea protection have actually questioned the importance of patents in *some* cases; others merely question the timing as to when people should search and/or apply.

The intent here is to address and evaluate the varying needs for certain forms of protection. Ultimately, you may elect to obtain a patent or you may determine this process to be wholly unnecessary. There are many competent and reputable patent attorneys who may differ with our findings. Not being attorneys, we must defer to the professional legal advice of such attorneys.

However, let us also say this about our own competency; we are in the front lines, dealing with thousands of everyday people with ideas that today are thriving. Some are patented, but more than half are not. It just either wasn't necessary at their own particular point of development or it wasn't necessary at all. Do not spend twenty-thousand dollars on legal fees to protect a worthless idea

If you are familiar with the history of United States, you know that it was founded, built, based upon and designed to support one primary force; a force that built the U.S.—the courageous dreamer. Just as the life-blood of any business is new business, the survival and growth of any country is based upon new ideas somehow evolved out of the old. Many countries want to protect and insure your concepts because they know their survival depends on you.

Yes, you might need protection, especially for a highly technical enterprise, and it might cost you quite a bit. But for a great majority, your cost for initial U.S. government protection is around $10.00, which is about the cost of a disclosure document registration fee and which generally establishes your origination date and basic protection for the first two years of your venture.

The Law of Protection and the Law of Human Nature

What is protection law and what rights does it entitle you to? The word "first" is the primary issue here. The idea of protection law is to establish and prove that you were the first to come up with your idea. But just because you have established such a precedent, doesn't guarantee you protection even if someone does allegedly steal or extrapolate from your genius. First you might have to sue, and you might not win. Unfortunately, that's the reality of the protection law today, otherwise there would be only one computer manufacturer, one fast-food chain, one brand of car.

The entire system contradicts itself unless you consider the foundations of free enterprise: competition and marketing, marketing, marketing! Corporate giants and a host of wealthy venturers can sometimes spend the money to protect some of their most valued concepts, which often causes a technological detente in those circles.

But you should be encouraged and not discouraged because if you have proven yourself to be first and a giant steals your idea, there are many attorneys who might love to represent you on a contingency fee. So corporations try to be careful not to knowingly lift ideas that belong to others. As you will learn, many corporations have specific submission procedures that require certain releases to protect themselves.

And you should be encouraged by the millions of ideas that are evolving daily at various stages, as well as the thousands of new ideas that crop up each week in so many forms. Again, a great majority of these endeavors are not patented but are protected by one crucial and underlying factor: momentum. These dreamers, builders, inventors, manufacturers and retailers are working on their ideas, making them grow and earning, by their efforts, a solid piece of the pie.

As we work to maximize your results on minimal budgets, you'll not only save a great deal of money, but you'll also give your idea a much greater chance of succeeding. In all our years of consulting, we have never found magic or instant easy money. Everything takes work and must be earned, and what we have often learned are better ways to work and deliver more effective results. Momentum—your best defense is the correct marketing offense. Keep that in mind as we systematically examine the various forms of protection you need first.

"What's this $10.00 Thing?"

Each and every week, thousands of people simply assume that they will immediately require a patent and do one of four things:

1. They discover it might cost over $1,000.00 and proceed.
2. They discover it might cost over $1,000.00 and give up on their entire idea.
3. They merely proceed without any protection.
4. They file a disclosure. The simple disclosure process which, providing you are indeed first, will protect you for the first two years of your venture—giving you time to generate revenue for a patent-pending application (around $185.00), a patent search and, finally, a patent or whatever else you may need at that time.

How Do I File a Disclosure Document?

To file a disclosure document, send duplicate photo's, illustrations, diagrams, written information, etc., with a self-addressed stamped envelope to:

The Commissioner of Patents and Trademarks
Washington, D.C. 20231

Be sure to include your $10.00 fee for each concept or process you wish to register. Remember, the disclosure document is not a patent and does not offer you the protection as such, but it's sometimes the best first step until you're certain that you need a patent.

Straight Talk about Patents

There are basically three types of patents:

1) **Plant** - for the protection of any new plant, tree, vegetable, etc.
2) **Design** - for the protection of decorative and/or visual outer "aesthetic" properties of any item, but not the internal core frame or structure.
3) **Function or Utility** - to protect mechanical designs and functions, most specifically in regard to inventions.

There are well over 100,000 patents awarded each year and well over a hundred thousand patent applications made each year. Unfortunately, a patent is often all that people ever get for their ideas.

There is another interesting statistic of which you might not be aware. Each week, approximately 50,000 new at-home businesses are begun and another 30,000+ new general businesses are started. What this means is that merely looking at the number of patent-applicants is deceiving. There are literally millions of people trying to get their piece of the pie working, or they may be stuck at various levels of progress.

Getting a patent is a tough process. If you do indeed require a patent, there are many competent attorneys who know all the right steps to take. So if you are convinced, or even if you are not certain, following legal advice is a valuable resource to help you best address the issue. If you are looking for a patent attorney to guide you, the least expensive procedure is a free consultation with a patent attorney for a half-hour. This is available through the American Intellectual Property Law Association's Inventor Consultation Service. For further information on this service, contact:

✉ The American Intellectual Property Law Association
2001 Jefferson Davis Highway Suite 203
Arlington, VA 22202

For further information on Patents and Patents Pending, contact:

✉ Department of Congress
Patent Office
2021 Jefferson Davis Highway Bldg. #3
Arlington, VA 20231

☎ Phone (703) 557-4636

What Does Having a Patent Mean?

Let's assume you have visited a patent attorney and she quotes the various options that protection laws may provide for you—maybe in a similar fashion as we have done so far in this chapter. Suppose she then says, "Okay, it's up to you, what do you want?" What are you then supposed to do?

To be extra-cautious, your attorney might insist on your beginning with the maximum patent-protection available under the law. After all, the purpose for creating patent, trademark and copyright laws are to support and encourage your creativity. While we often find ourselves in similar positions regarding patent questions and often make referrals to patent attorneys, we hope this chapter leaves you with more of an understanding of what your actual options are as we enter the new millennium. We hope that you will keep the basic intent of the protection laws in mind—to not let your good ideas die and to find the best way to bring your idea(s) to life.

We have worked with many unpatented products as well as many patented ones. Ultimately, you'll have to decide where your resources and hard-earned money will be best utilized. The following connection exercise may assist you.

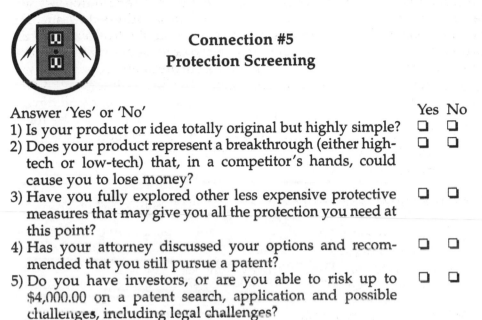

Connection #5
Protection Screening

Answer 'Yes' or 'No'

	Yes	No
1) Is your product or idea totally original but highly simple?	❑	❑
2) Does your product represent a breakthrough (either high-tech or low-tech) that, in a competitor's hands, could cause you to lose money?	❑	❑
3) Have you fully explored other less expensive protective measures that may give you all the protection you need at this point?	❑	❑
4) Has your attorney discussed your options and recommended that you still pursue a patent?	❑	❑
5) Do you have investors, or are you able to risk up to $4,000.00 on a patent search, application and possible challenges, including legal challenges?	❑	❑

If you have answered yes to more than one of these questions, you probably should seriously consider pursuing a patent. However, if a disclosure-document, which essentially protects your venture for its first two years and only costs around $10.00, will suffice until you have proven to yourself and perhaps your associates that your concept will make money, then you should seriously consider that as your first option.

How Do I Submit an Idea to a Corporation?

Some companies charge sizable fees just to supposedly shape your concept and then present it to the appropriate industry. You come up with the idea, pay one of these brokers some money, and bingo, you're rich! Don't you wish that were true? It is, of course, not true for most cases. What is true is that most companies, large and small, have their own parameters for agreeing to review your idea.

Most companies are built on ideas and need new ones or improvements upon old ones in order to thrive and survive. So most companies do have their own internal research and development organization dedicated to monitoring and meeting the needs of their product or service line. But every once in a while, someone like you comes along with an idea, and while a high percentage of these ideas won't be accepted by these companies, some do spark interest. Your best bet for submitting an idea to a company, via its proper guidelines, is to contact that company and ask them to send you their conditions for agreeing to review your idea. That's where you start. You may find that some companies won't even glance at your idea unless you have a patent—others are not as stringent. A good tip is to begin by seeking out smaller-sized manufacturers/distributors with a relevant product or service line.

Please note that the more preliminary and low-cost research and development you undertake, the better prepared your concept will be for a presentation to the company.

Non-Disclosure

Smaller, local companies are generally more receptive and often easier to work with, but again, it depends upon their abilities to work effectively with your idea. Most of you will want to make sure that after submitting your idea no one will use it without your authorization. Sometimes you will produce non-disclosure forms or contracts that resemble something like the form on this page.

However, what you might not be prepared for is that some companies will sign your non-disclosure form and some won't. Almost all will have their own protection form for you to sign, which essentially states that, while they may agree to look at or discuss your idea, their research department may have already thought of the idea long before you did. And if that's true, they won't want you to come after them for an idea they actually thought up first. One gets the impression that it's just a matter of the old principal, "you just have to trust someone," and since most long-term business is built on trust, you may have to take a chance like that.

Again, if you're still not sure, let your attorney have the last word. Get a second or even a third legal opinion (all free, if possible) before you commit to any legal expenditure. While we have learned a great deal about protection laws in this country, we do not have the legal training or certification of a qualified and reputable attorney. Our expertise is in protecting you by helping you to find the most viable ways to produce and market your concept—protection through the strength, power and earnings of sales.

Trademarks and Copyrights

First, we'll explore the Trademark or Service Mark because, as with patent issues, trademarks are still under the auspices of the commissioner of Patents and Trademarks in the U.S. Department of Commerce

🖹 A Non-Disclosure Form

> I, _____, on this date _____ do
> hereby submit to _____ for the pur-
> pose of reviewing my idea which in general terms, is agreed by
> both parties that it can be described as:
>
> _____
>
> _____
>
> _____
>
> _____
>
> The reviewer(s) of this idea and their companies and associates
> agree **not** to copy, utilize, manufacture, or make use of in any way,
> this idea without express written consent from me. It is further
> agreed that if said reviewer(s) do utilize my idea in any way, I shall
> be compensated via mutually agreeable terms.
>
> Signed, _____
> Your Name & Company
>
> Signed, _____
> Reviewer(s)
>
> Date _____

(Note: If you're utilizing this manual outside of the U.S., please refer to
your country's own protection system, and/or U.S. International patent
law).

The simplest way to explain what a trademark is would be to say
"Coca-Cola," "IBM," etc. A trademark is a word, logo, symbol, or any
generally visual device, imprinted on each and every product or packaging of any service to indicate ownership, origination, quality and
identity as it relates to publicity and advertising.

Trademarks, built-up over time, can be worth a great deal of money and
cannot be copied or used without permission. A trademark or service
mark symbol protects the right and ownership but does not, in itself,

prevent others from making or selling the concept, as does a patent and patent-pending.

Just as a lawyer will conduct a patent search to assure potential originality of your idea, there is a Trademark register of the United States available in most libraries. Similar to a patent search via satellite patent offices, you can save money and make sure your trademark is indeed original by conducting your own trademark search. You can register any of your own original trademarks providing:

- ☑ They do not depict anything suggesting deception, immorality, disrespect for persons living or dead regarding any individual beliefs.
- ☑ They do not depict signature or portrait of a deceased United States president, as long as the widow is still alive, unless she grants permission for such use.
- ☑ No flag or coat of arms may be used or incorporated.
- ☑ No common mainstream language term is used.

Copyrights

The key issue of a copyright is that it prevents someone from copying those written works which you originated. Believe it or not, a copyright is your protective right against being copied. Copyrights are inexpensive (usually under $10.00) and are geared to protecting original works of authorship. If someone should attempt to use anything you have originally written without your permission, and you do wind up in court, the law recognizes your copyright as legal proof of your origination.

Examples of copyrightable material are:

- Manuals
- Photographs
- Seminar guides and other guides and the actual presentations
- Original descriptions of original products.
- Books
- Sound recordings
- Software
- Graphic design
- Most advertising and/or promotional presentations via most mediums (print, radio and TV)

Certain everyday symbols, such as stop signs, slogans, phrases, etc., and other related issues, cannot be copyrighted.

A copyright gives the processed applicant full ownership and exclusive rights to handle or sell that material.

For complete details, including copyright applications, contact:

✉ Copyright Office
Library of Congress
Washington, D.C. 20559

☎ (202) 707-9100

📄 For further information on Copyrights, request publication 'R-2'

📄 To copyright a standard book, booklet or most written items, request form 'TX'

To summarize, the law *wants* to protect the creator, originator, inventor or pioneer, and indeed there are laws to protect virtually anything you can dream of creating. Just remember that you are always better off if you're part of the sales-chain. Because even if you do have your protection in place and launch a lawsuit which can cost a lot of money, the suit might not be heard for several years, and then you could lose.

Dear *me*

✉ Many people ask about postmarking a written form of an idea. In other words, paying your local post office first class stamp cost so they will affix that day's postal imprint, complete with date. Again, with a good lawyer and a sympathetic jury, this might be accepted. It could, however, be useful if your competitor is small-time and you show them your stamp. This information also regards the doing business certificates available in most city or town halls.

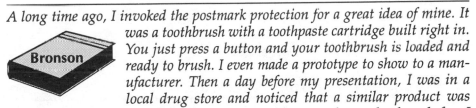

A long time ago, I invoked the postmark protection for a great idea of mine. It was a toothbrush with a toothpaste cartridge built right in. You just press a button and your toothbrush is loaded and ready to brush. I even made a prototype to show to a manufacturer. Then a day before my presentation, I was in a local drug store and noticed that a similar product was already on the market. I later found out it had been on the market long before I ever thought of it.

So copyright, patent-pend and trademark when you can, but be fairly certain about a patent before you proceed. Most importantly, channel your energies into getting your idea developed and marketed. If you focus on listening to the needs of your market, produce a reliable and good quality product or service, and remain determined and focused about where and how you work, you should be able to earn, keep, and even grow a marketshare.

It is deceptive for anyone to say that any particular protection or sales methodology is a guarantee for money. A patent is no guarantee for cash, nor is an ad, etc. But if you'll work hard and follow these steps, I believe you'll succeed and you'll discover that your best guarantee is directly contingent upon your own sales initiative.

Now, back to our regularly scheduled chapter...

Summary

Now that we have our blueprint or general performance plans, it's time to create some form of prototype or functional guide. If you've followed the steps to this point, your concept should have sufficient clarity to relate well to your initial subjects.

1) Bring the Idea into a Tangible Form

❑ Create an initial model.

2) Implement Low-Cost Ways to Utilize Effective Resources

❑ Locate and organize resources to assemble a detailed model and/or written proposal.
❑ If any fees are involved, get a full understanding of what they are in advance.
❑ Be extremely clear when telling any artists or other vendors what you are looking for.
❑ Continually check on progress.

3) Pursue Protection if Necessary

❑ Send your idea to yourself and your lawyer to obtain postmark as proof of your idea origination date.

❏ File a disclosure document with The Commissioner of Patents and Trademarks.
❏ Investigate if you need a patent at this time.
  ❏ Complete Connection #4 - Protection Screening
  ❏ Get free consultation from patent attorney.
❏ Obtain a trademark or copyright for your idea.
❏ Prepare to submit your idea to a corporation.
  ❏ Create a non-disclosure agreement.

Potential Challenges and Solutions

Challenge: Can't make a model.

Solution: If you feel you just can't put together some kind of model or written description, you may need to do more homework. With sufficient knowledge, you should be able to put something together if you're really serious about your idea.

Re-examine your sources. Someone may be giving you misleading or unqualified advice which is creating an obstacle for you.

Challenge: Can't get anything on paper.

Solution: Even if you're barely literate, if you can relate any thoughts to other people, you can find help to get those words clearly on paper. Break through this fear and give your venture a chance to succeed.

Before You Continue...

❏ Have you found a means to create a working demonstration of your idea?
❏ Are you continuing to find ways to advance instead of excuses to stop?
❏ Are you seeking out qualified critics/consultants?
❏ Are you listening constructively?

Chapter Five

First Steps to Market
Materializing Your Concept

> *"An idea isn't worth much until someone with dedication makes it work."*
>
> **William Feather**

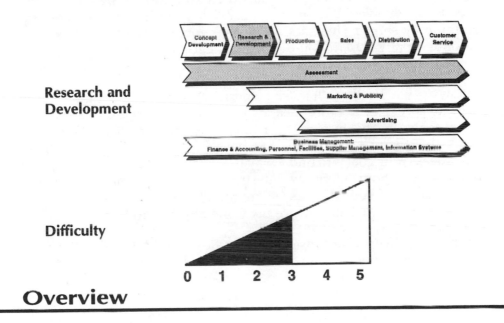

Research and Development

Difficulty

Overview

Even more important than testing is evaluation of data. This requires careful listening, and especially, potential buyers. Actively seek out critics and be grateful for their valuable time and input.

Action Steps

1) Incorporate feedback.
2) Earn and learn each step of the way.
3) Present your concept.

1) Incorporate Feedback

Based upon our research and your prior input, Power-Up Tip #2 in Chapter 4 should address the battery of protection issues for most of you, hence, giving you the impetus to carry on with your research and development.

At this point, you're actively seeking out the experts in relevant fields who will spend some free time giving you their opinions. At these meetings, expect to be insulted occasionally. After all, your concept is a part of you, but you're looking for hardcore critiques now before any big expense is involved. Write down a list of hard questions. Let them rip your idea to shreds. They may finally kick you out. They may make you an offer. In any case, if you do as much ego-free listening as possible, you will invariably leave these encounters with more than you came.

Whatever you hear, you'll make no decision at this point. You may now want to forget your entire idea, or you may want to jump at the first offer you've heard. Instead, go home, or go back to work and don't think about your venture for a few days. Then, slowly digest all these new ideas. Your goal is to find a way to make your idea more viable and to advance it. Some of you will destroy your original models and proposals. Some of you will make slight modifications. In either case, you will be finding ways to enhance the value of your product.

Keep it fun. Keep your sense of humor. Revel in the fact that throughout our career, we have already made the big mistakes for you. You have reached this crucial development stage without spending any significant money. Discouragement can and will be corrected, but a squandered life-savings over a half-tested idea? You can avoid that.

We've seen it happen to people of all levels of intelligence. We wish they had the sense to invest a few dollars in this book. Think of the money they could have saved, and that's not the only loss. Their wonderful idea becomes only a bitter memory.

So no matter what stage you're at (and many of you will have suffered severe setbacks at this stage of the game), it doesn't matter. What does matter is the heightened awareness and education you now have about your idea. Your small failures are crucial for paving the way to a more genuine success. Young or old, you don't have time to mourn your mistakes. Just learn from them and move forward. Remember, regret is the greatest waste of human resources!

A few years ago, one of my first cousins was dying of an inoperable brain tumor. He was a physician who was always trying to make a better widget. One of his final projects was the development of a more efficient tissue-analysis unit.

Bronson

Even in his final weeks of life, he was busily trying to get this project going. His wife is now putting the finishing touches on his invention. Motivation begets enthusiasm, enthusiasm begets energy and keeps us alive. What's your excuse? Don't give up on an idea with potential. You may have to re-channel your energies a bit. You may even want to walk away from it all for a week or two. Take a mental vacation from it until you can approach it with a fresh attitude.

As writers, we love our computer/word processor because it allows us to correct the same page as many times as necessary without any extra effort or time. We can give the impression of being able to take criticism well for any of our writing because the word processor permits us to perfect our product without the traditional labor and frustration. Ego-free listening and the pursuit of excellence becomes easier all the time.

The point is not to get a computer, but to patiently rework your model until the experts love it. That way you get the experts' stamp of approval, but you still own the idea! By sticking with our planning and development advice, you've created some exciting options for yourself. You didn't sell out, so as a reward, you can now offer potential players the option of "buying in." Now you've got something, and Chapter 6 will help you begin to make the best of it in some very exciting and profitable ways.

Perfect 10 Test

"Don't tell me I need tests. I know this is a great idea. This is me; this is my child, my baby. I haven't felt this strongly about an idea in years. We'll make thousands of them right away. Wait a minute... babies learn by falling. Maybe I'd better go a little more slowly here."

Smart person, whoever spoke those above words. Does it describe you also? Are you anxious or enthusiastic? Are you listening well, and are you evaluating what you've learned and incorporating it properly into your mental model?

That's good but even if you feel comfortable and have done batteries of sophisticated tests, nothing will save you more money and heartache like the real perfect 10 test.

Most of you are proceeding cautiously out of necessity, but some of you are reading this while nervously wondering what can be done to unload a warehouse full of unsold items you made or stocked up on. Well, sometimes we can develop ways to move those items, but hopefully you've learned an important lesson that you'll remember forever; in most cases, do not manufacture too far ahead of your demand and keep watching your market for changes and incorporate those changes into your product. Moreover, always remember the perfect 10 test.

We all know that, aside from the one we love, there's no such thing as the perfect 10. But now let me tell you about another perfect 10; one that can save you loads of money and even save your business from complete disaster. Most importantly, the '10' test can preserve the vitality of your dream. You are at this point in the book because you have researched, conceptualized, re-worked, re-conceptualized and possibly protected your concept to the point where you think you are ready to go into production. There is one more crucial step which you shall be using throughout the life of your idea—the model and/or the test. If your idea involves a service, start small—don't over commit. If it's a product and you've made a model that seems to work well, still, for your first production run, make ten. That's it—just 10. We will be discussing models, prototypes and pre-production planning, but progress is determined much less by luck and far more by gradual testing and evaluation that begins on the smallest scale possible. Especially those first ten units.

2) Earn and Learn Each Step of the Way

Whenever we are personally involved in the development of a product, after we are satisfied with our model, we then attempt to make ten perfect prototypes. The prototypes are exact replicas of what we believe will finally be in distribution, with possibly the exception of packaging (since certain retail or other sales may require varying forms of packaging).

We then present these prototypes to prospective distributors, as if we are presenting any product for a sale. The distributors we approach are usually the biggies, i.e. the ones who would buy in the largest quantities. Hopefully, if we are polite and professional in our approach, this prospective buyer will respond honestly with one of the most vital components you'll ever get for your idea—professional criticism. If the buyer says no, find out why. What changes could you make to make him say yes?

Of course, as we've indicated earlier, don't exclude your local retail market. Those down-home responses can teach you as much as any others. Are you beginning to see the value of the perfect ten test? Before you over-manufacture or over-commit, these buyers could give you the most valuable advice you could ever hope for.

Testing addresses and hopefully solves simple issues before those issues become major problems. *It's better and, in fact, it's okay to make a thousand mistakes in your testing phase as opposed to even one mistake in thousands of an untested item.*

Power-Up Tip #3
Why Do We Test and
What Do We Test for?

1) Safety

- ❏ Has it met, or preferably exceeded, all safety standards as required by all pertinent laws and codes in all designated sales areas?
- ❏ Apart from legal requirements, can you anticipate potential safety issues, exclusive to your concept that must be addressed?
- ❏ Have you addressed as many safety problems as you can possibly think of before you allow anyone to actually try your concept?

2) Manufacturing

- ❏ Are you using the most appropriate materials?
- ❏ Is your assembly/manufacturing process the most efficient, economical and hazard-free?
- ❏ If possible, are you utilizing biodegradable materials?

3) Function

- ❏ Does your product work consistently and repeatedly?
- ❏ Can your service deliver what you promise it will?
- ❏ Is your product designed to last for an amount of time comparable to or in excess of the competition?

4) Response

- ❏ Has your target market indicated interest?
- ❏ Have you incorporated legitimate suggestions into your concept?
- ❏ Can you produce your concept at promised price and still make a profit?

5) Price

❑ Is your price competitive?
❑ Can you test at different pricing levels?

Service and Needs

Everyone used to joke about selling refrigerators to Eskimos, but today, many modern Eskimos have refrigerators, just like anyone else. So to apply the 10 test to a service idea, you must take much of what you have learned about the need for your service from the previous chapters. What percentage of the population would utilize this service? Will there be competition? Could you try out your idea first through just an ad in the local paper or yellow pages? Again, determine response and demand, and then respond and progress accordingly. Do not go right into an office space without first taking a step-by-step process of determining if the population will support your idea, or if you can sufficiently market your service in order to make your venture profitable.

Getting to "Yes"

*"Almost anything can become a **yes** if you listen carefully enough as to why you got a **no**."*

A negative response is only a temporary learning phase to a genuine small businessperson. Of course, as indicated earlier, the responses are a bit more detailed. If you are fortunate enough to get a positive response, what does that actually mean? And does a no really mean no way? The key will be finding what is wrong and how to correct it. Did you speak to the right person? Were they too busy? Always get to the core of your mistakes so you can progress.

You shall be referring to the upcoming "Connection" chart throughout many phases of the development of your concept. It is designed to aid you in making clear-cut analysis to enable you to get closer to a sale. Moreover, to conserve our financial and other resources, we are always looking for the shortest distance to a sale or the promise (letter of intent) of same.

Hopefully, before you even talk to a prospect, you will study this chart so as to get an idea of what you are aiming for. Right after the chart, we shall explore the current state of your concept and what we will have to do before we give your idea a test-run.

Finding the Decision-Maker

You will notice in Connection #6 that the terms 'buyer' and 'prospect' are frequently used, but in fact, there are many labels your prospect may assume. Be sure you are speaking to, or eventually will speak to, a genuine decision-maker who has money and authority to commit. If it will be a committee decision, can you meet with the entire committee?

Hundreds of New Prospects Are Created Daily

Every day, hundreds of new prospects are created—new items, new stores or services that may be ideal match-ups for your service. So how do you find the right buyers? There are several ways:

Starting Small

The first place I ever sold my book, 'Good Idea! Now What?' was in a local, independently-owned hardware store, since I theorized that a lot of do-it-yourself types would appreciate the intent of the book. The local owner/buyer agreed to try ten on consignment—and they sold within a matter of days. From then on, he bought on a cash basis.

Are there local shops which can prominently display your product? It's a good, inexpensive way to test your idea and build your sales-confidence. Then, if your item will do well in a few local stores, how do you reach hundreds or even thousands of similar stores?

There are so many ways to link up and interconnect with the various sales avenues, and not just on the retail level, as we will learn. However, if you have created a successful local retail test and want to expand, there are two viable ways to approach this:

Back-Tracing

Who sold the local store the major products they sell? What distributors did they deal with? Pick a product or products that, while not identical or specifically competitive, could be sold to the same retailers which yours could be—a similar family of items, so to speak. Now *back-trace*. Who sold those items to the retailer? Ask the retailer for the name of the distributors who may be relevant to your concept.

Directories

While back-tracing is a very powerful vehicle to help get you started, the ever-expanding and ever-changing world of reps, distributors and buyers is a vast and often complicated one; so, don't over-commit to any rep or distributor unless you have some evidence of their capabilities (and the freedom to fire them if they don't do their intended job!). If you are seeking a more systematic approach in your retail distribution hunt, check the following sources:

1) For **self-employment organizations**, contact:

≡' National Association for the Self-Employed
2121 Precinct Line Rd.
Hurst, TX 76054
☎ (800) 232-6273

2) For **Retail & Distributor** Information, contact:

≡' The National Retail Merchants Association
325 7th Street NW
Suite 1000
Washington, DC 20004
☎ (202) 783-7971

3) Another good provider of important listings of **prospective distributors**, via specific retail categories is:

≡' The National Association of Chain Drug Stores
Box 1417-D49
Alexandria, VA 22313
☎ (703) 549-3001

4) If you are seeking to present to **manufacturers**, go to your local library and utilize the Thomas Register of American Manufacturers from:

≡' Thomas Publishing Company
One Penn Plaza
New York, NY 10119
☎ (212) 695-0500

As with many, this is a very expensive directory (about $180.00), so always check your local library first! And if your local library doesn't have it, maybe they could order it.

You may or may not be ready to make use of the above associations and directories, but if you are ready to use the upcoming Yes Chart, you should then have a broad base of target (prospective) markets to hone in on. My experience has been that no does not always mean 'no,' but more usually, it means not yet or not under either the terms or the conditions which you have presented your item to me.

3) Present Your Concept

"How Far Along Should I Go Before Making a Presentation?" That obviously depends upon a lot of circumstances, including your own personal capabilities and relevancy to the idea. Suffice to say, the more professional your presentation, the better chance you will have of being taken seriously.

When my partner and I presented our video-conferencing concept in preparation for and at the international business plan competition (see Chapter 3), we simulated the video-conferencing concept. I would sit in a room adjoining the audience room in front of a video camera. The video image was sent via cable to a screen in the main presentation room where my partner would lead the presentation. The audience was free to ask questions of either one of us, and we would respond appropriately.

In the two situations in which we performed this simulation, the audience was shocked to learn that I was in the next room. During the presentation, they thought I was across town or even in another state. Needless to say, we were taken very seriously, and our points about the benefits of the service we were proposing were obvious.

"I'm Petrified. I'm Not a Salesperson."

Yes you are. In one way or another, everyone has to represent themselves at some level just to survive. All selling requires is honesty and a willingness to listen and learn. Don't force; let your product do the selling. Moreover, as far as confidence is concerned, you'll earn it as you learn about your concept and its market.

Connection #6
The Yes Chart. A Simple,
Systematic Approach for Closing a Sale

How are you approaching your prospects?
❑ Wholesale ❑ Retail ❑ Direct Mail

Use the chart on the next page to assist in your initial order closing steps.

Step	If 'Yes'...	If 'No'...
1) What is the response to your initial presentation? Will the prospect issue an order or P.O.?	**Product** Quantity = _____ Payable in ____ days **Service** Quantity = _____ (hours, days, weeks, months) Payable at $ _____ Per _____ (h,d,w,m) Go to Step 2.	List conditions needed to get an order or purchase order: _____ _____ _____ _____ Return to Step 1.
2) Can P.O. be cancelled?	Under what terms? _____ _____ Go to Step 3.	Excellent! Go to Step 3.
3) Can you receive a non-refundable down payment?	Excellent! Get it. Go to Step 4.	Ask again. It can't hurt. Go to Step 4.
4) Is this a consignment order whereby you are paid only on items sold?	Go to Step 5.	Go to the bank! Go to Step 5.
5) If you have followed sequence and still have no sale, is product or service sufficiently presentable for buyer?	Go to Step 6.	Ask prospect what improvements are needed? Have you left too much up to the buyer's imagination? Return to Step 1.
6) Are you courting the wrong market, prospect or buyer?	Get focused! Return to Step 1.	Go to Step 7.
7) Is your competition offering a better product at better terms?	Rethink your price and/or improve your product. Return to Step 1.	Go to Step 8.
8) Did the product / service sell itself, or did you sell the product / service too forcefully?	Slow down! Believe in yourself and your idea. Return to Step 1.	Try again. Return to Step 1.

Test Progress Notes:

Date   Action and/or Follow-through

_____

_____

_____

_____

_____

_____

_____

_____

_____

_____

_____

_____

_____

_____

_____

_____

Summary

In this chapter, your new feedback will often come from many of your potential buyers, who often become your unwitting production associates, as they will often tell you exactly what you'll need to do to get them to buy, invest or distribute your concept. Many giant leaps are often made in this chapter.

1) Incorporate Feedback

❑ Use the 'Perfect 10' concept.
❑ Progress effectively, but with minimal risk.

2) Earn and Learn Each Step of the Way

❑ Shape your concept to potential buyers, distributors, etc.
❑ Make them your most valuable ally.
❑ Take note of Power-Up Tip #3.
❑ Investigate prospect sources:
    ❑ Local outlets
    ❑ Back-tracing
    ❑ Directories
    ❑ Find the decision-makers.

3) Present Your Concept

❑ Actively seek out and listen to their best criticism.
❑ Research-Refine-Research-Refine.
❑ Get to 'Yes' with the assistance of Connection #6.
❑ Keep increasing the value of your product and service.

Potential Challenges and Solutions

Challenge: Can't seem to muster resources to generate any kind of interest.

Solution: If your heart's in the right idea, you won't stop until you've actively sought out those resources that can assist you. Are you seeking out critics?

Challenge: Can't find the means to make my concept into something real and functional.

Solution: Coming up with something new requires a great deal of creative thinking, of which we all are capable. Look at the same old possibilities in new ways. Also, since large ventures generally begin with a single seed of a notion, how can you find the new doors that will carry your concept forward?

Before You Continue...

❑ Is your concept a by-product of disciplined motivation or careless over-anxiousness?
❑ Are you listening well to your team players?
❑ Have you approached a potential review or sale with confidence?
❑ Do you now have new ways to increase your concept's value?

Chapter Six

Testing the Market
Making It Go without Letting It Go

> *"Ideas are like children. There are none so wonderful as your own."*
>
> **Fortune Cookie**

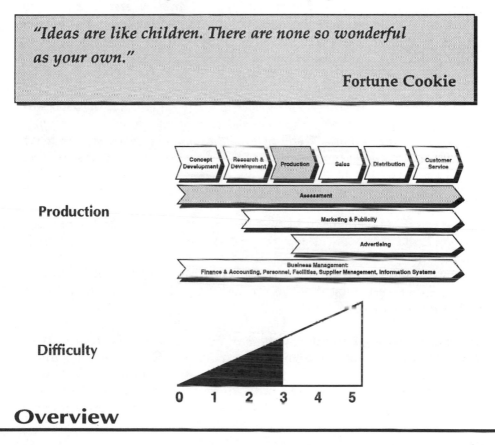

Overview

This is an exciting stage where you will not only be seeking out potential distributors, manufacturers or various other buyers, you will also be soliciting their strongest critiques. In essence, the very people you are going to sell to are going to tell you exactly what you need to do to get them to commit.

Action Steps

1) Maximize your concept's value.
2) Present your prototype to the market.
3) Create inexpensive resources.

1) Maximize Your Concept's Value

A few years ago, I witnessed the installation of the latest high-tech desalinization machinery at a popular Caribbean resort. Years of lab research had yielded the ultimate device for turning sea water into the purest drinking water imaginable, "Purer and tastier than spring water," as its developers told me.

They had a party to officially ordain this great machinery with gallons of converted water for all to test. Everyone seemed to have good things to say about this brilliantly engineered marvel. When they asked me for my opinion, I said the first thing that came to my mind, "It still tastes a little salty." Everyone laughed except for the inventors who later discovered that their device did indeed have a problem.

A few weeks and several thousand dollars later, it was corrected after much embarrassment and the most essential test of all—the people test. No matter how perfect the lab results, the word of that end-user is your best teacher. Our aims are to avoid salty public embarrassments while we continue progressing.

You have made strides in developing your idea and now have to face the challenge of testing it while building your own personal value to any future prospect.

Can you imagine giving up rights and ownership of your idea only to discover that someone else ended up making a fortune on it—and it made just a few pennies for you. You didn't think you were capable of making it happen, so you sold out. The multi-billion dollar Microsoft bought the original core DOS software for only $75,000 from someone who had a *Great Idea*. After you read this book, you should have an entirely new attitude about selling out.

A good buddy of mine in New York is a major television commercial producer. He proudly boasts a clientele that reads like a who's who from Fortune Magazine. You'd think he would be a multimillionaire with all those firms under his belt. In fact, he's barely making it and almost went bankrupt a few years ago.

He had Proposal Fever. His problem became clear to me and my associates one day when we waded through the piles of scattered papers just to walk into his office. There were full pages and random notes of extremely good ideas every-where, any single one worth thousands, if developed. But he was so enamored with the romance and excitement of the idea phase that he mailed his thoughts to every prospect he could think of. Very often, he would ask for nothing in return and often didn't even bother to follow-up on these great ideas.

Did corporations show interest in his proposals and ideas? Very often. Did he get paid or even recognized for these ideas? Not usually. He never learned to protect himself contractually and never learned the mechanics of the follow-up phases.

You don't have to be a non-professional to unwittingly give away all of your hard work. People at all levels get short-changed on their ideas to the tune of billions of dollars daily. Why do you think so many lawyers get rich? They often rake it in from the simple and avoidable mistakes.

Believe it or not, lawyers and good advice can become your best allies if used before the crisis erupts. A lot of you are afraid to pursue your *Great Idea* past the thrill of the romance stage. Seeing your concept at the model phase is primarily gratifying for your ego, but serves little other purpose toward your goal of marketing, control and profit, and self-actualization.

A lot of our new clients come to us as bitter people, convinced that mar-ket savvy and success can only happen to the other guy. So, they offer us hefty fees because they've either given up on their own talents, or they haven't read this book.

People become bitter when they try it the wrong way and then refuse to learn the right way. They become convinced that their way proves that the system doesn't work for them. If they had done it right, maybe we'd be out of jobs, but they would be happier people. There's nothing like participating in a success, but you must have incentive.

Much of our work involves keeping people excited by showing them the fruits of their efforts at each step. One should never underestimate the power of instilling incentive and confidence.

Lee Iacocca's incentive plans for Chrysler were so good, they were actu-ally greater than he was. Against his wishes, a strike in late 1985 was set-tled by paying his workers fees that gave them parity with competitive autoworkers. Iacocca was not terribly keen on the idea. He thought it would drain the company dry.

The strikers won and a month after settlement, the company posted some of their strongest earnings ever. His own philosophy of incentive triumphed. That which is perceived as an "Ultra-incentive" will produce Ultra-results. You will always keep your incentive in your pursuits because you will always create for yourself the proper involvement at each step. Never sell out unless you're talking fortunes and retirement. Even then it's nice to keep a hand in just in case you need the production resources.

In fact, you are going to learn to have more than just an interest. Your prospects and associates will realize that you are uniquely qualified to merit a controlling and supervisory interest. After all, it's your baby.

Don't Use the Dime-Store Approach

Your first premise is to never use the dime-store approach when selling your product. The dime-store approach entails taking a flat fee for a product or idea, then just walking away. You're paid a fee that may seem sizable to you at the time, then you go home and wash your hands of the whole thing. The idea has been so much a part of you and so important to you, and now you're just going to cash out? You've turned your dream into something that someone will buy from you. Sometimes the first-time thrill of that idea makes people lose their perspective.

An extremely persnickety client of mine gave birth to one of the first miniature home air-filtration systems. He was a scientist and knew very little about marketing. He sold out and then watched helplessly as his invention was picked apart, cheapened and rendered almost inoperative.

This bastardization of his brain-child nearly drove him crazy. This was his product. Subsequently, he marched into the bank, mortgaged his two homes to the hilt and bought back full rights to his products.

He redeveloped it and got it to market his way. After he had broken even and was well on his way to enjoying a tremendous bonanza, imitations began popping up all over the place, developed and distributed by major companies worldwide.

By the time he came to me, all the major producers and distributors were well on their way to burying him alive. He blew it by selling out in the first place so when it came time to legitimately utilize the services of a distributor, he refused to trust anyone but himself.

By not maintaining proper control, he had ultimately rendered his efforts obsolete. I'm sure I could have helped him if he had come to me earlier but when he finally did come to me, his only options were either to sell the company before it went bankrupt or to develop an entirely new idea. He streamlined his company and went back to the drawing board. He'll be back smarter and stronger, we hope.

The final decision is yours. If you want to just take the money and run, we can't stop you, but obviously, we don't advise it unless we're talking BIG bucks. Even then, as with the situation we just described, selling out may not be your best option.

What you have learned thus far has helped you to get started, but it's only the beginning. You're still caught in the thrill of a brand-new romance. Now comes the marriage.

You've brought your idea closer to perfection, and now you just can't wait to go back and show up your critics. You probably think that my next piece of advice is to make just such a presentation. You couldn't be more wrong.

You began with an idea and then you turned the abstract into something tangible, a product or service, at least twice critiqued and refined at this point. You started as a shaky dreamer. Then we transformed you into a researcher, an inventor, a designer and a developer. That's quite a company you're becoming.

We've worked hard to increase the value of you and your company. You may indeed go back to a manufacturer or distributor and work with them. You'll ultimately have to make the best determination for you and your venture. After this chapter, your options should clarify.

"Sell-Out" Caution

If you're thinking of becoming a "sell-out," be aware that many ideas are purchased and are then never released. Companies often buy out competitive ideas just to crush any potential competition. So if you do sell out, do one of two things:
  1) Get a production commitment which will return the rights of your idea to you after an agreed period of time if the buyer does not produce and sell it, or
  2) Get a GENEROUS sum of money.

Or, as you have already observed, many ideas die from a simple case of misdirection. The bottom line is—don't let your good ideas die for any price. The world always needs better ways to do things. Your idea could make a difference.

On to the Market

So where do you go from here? How about to the marketplace. That's right; you read it right. All you have is a rough, refined prototype. You're in the infancy of production stages, yet we are going to expose you to the marketplace.

You are about to undergo what is commonly known as a market test. You've gotten samples in the mail of new products. That type of promotion or test can cost millions, and what if the product has to be modified? The cheapest market surveys can cost thousands of dollars even before you know if your product is ready.

You don't want to spend that kind of money on your project, but would you be willing to invest under ten dollars plus a little time to test your idea?

Remember Hitchcock. We have to find out how the public and related industries feel about what we're up to. We have our legal protection and research behind us. Let's find out what the world is 'theeenking.' You may already have a distributor and/or manufacturer in mind. Wouldn't it be simple just to build that relationship and move ahead? Be advised, there may be several people out there who can help your product come to life. Don't limit yourself to one chance prospect.

**Connection #7
Describing Your Idea**

Here's your assignment; write three paragraphs describing the features and benefits of your idea. Is it new? Say so and explain what it does that may render existing competitors obsolete. Don't explain how. Don't be too technical and don't give away too many hints about your research conclusions. And, by all means, always include at least a mailing address and preferably a phone number.

Convey that your product is available for distribution or participation (if appropriate). This is done to officiate and lend credibility to your product or service. DO NOT EVER LIE about your product. Genuine advertising is a responsibility to the public to tell the truth in an attractive and appealing manner.

I'm sure you have noticed that some of the most outrageous claims are made for some of the most inferior products. The harder someone tries to sell something to me, the more dubious you should become. Don't promise magic, just better features and benefits than the others (and you'd better have better features than the others!). Write something that you would believe yourself. Run it by some friends. We're not looking for cute copy. Cute is dangerous if not used skillfully—"just the facts, ma'am."

Is your writing understandable? Can people get an idea of what your product is about just from your paragraphs? Have you created curiosity? Spend a week writing if you need to, but no more than that. Don't get stuck. We write these types of descriptions all of the time and my blurbs appear in hundreds of magazines each year. Since we've been doing them for years, we can usually churn them out in less than an hour. Ultimately, you'll be able to do the same thing. You should be able to write as fast as you can clearly relate your ideas in ordinary conversation.

Now that you have produced this press release, the trick is to get the message to the right people. This book is laced with the common theme of bringing each task to a successful conclusion. This is both exhilarating and terrifying for many of you who never dreamed they would see anything of theirs in print. You'll soon discover how easy it can be. Nothing is easy until you master it, but if you've made it this far, you can make it the rest of the way. Many of you don't believe it, and we used to lose a lot of promising students at this stage. It's easy to get stuck right before your big debut. Let's continue on...but first these important words from your sponsors...

Power-Up Tip #4
DON'T GET STUCK
There's Always a Way

Ideas die when people don't know what to do next to move them forward. It happens all the time. Ignorance and lack of confidence are the leading cause of death among promising ventures. Even business professionals can be afraid to admit that certain delays are caused by procedural ignorance, so all you hear from them are excuses and stories. Pride or fear of job security shields ignorance and the idea falls victim.

Good business health is determined by any measurable signs of moving forward. Even when struggling, people who dedicate themselves to making their product move ahead are rarely depressed.

Keep it going. If you don't know, ask, learn. If you have a problem, solve it. There's always an economical, ethical and effective way.

As we were putting this book together, some of our critics told us to cut any words of encouragement and just stick to the "How To Stuff." This was one time when we found our critics to be dead wrong. The world is full of "How To" encyclopedias on how to do anything, but with little sympathy for how you, the reader, is thinking. So instead of learning "How To" with many of these books, you learn "How NOT To" once you run up against your first inhuman directive that you don't understand. You learn "how not to" permanently by creating fear and lack of confidence as your biggest enemies. The success of your venture is a highly personal issue, and we want no one to be left behind.

We can't get too heavy, and we can't play psychologist. All we can say is that, if you're stuck, there's always a way to get unstuck. Find it.

To those of you who are now ready to move forward, go get em! You're going to encounter a lot of characters who might try to raise your blood pressure and steal your sleep and worse. Our intention is to not have you lose a single night's sleep.

You see, it doesn't make any difference what kind of characters approach you, we'll teach you how to deal with them. You'll have the control and the upper hand. If anyone loses sleep, it'll be the other guy, not you.

Fear no one. This is your game and you make the final rules. Alas, there is still a segment of you who have never finished a "How To" book or any venture, for that matter. You began with the best of intentions and hopes, but then repeated the same old pattern of fear and failure, like a worm crawling around the inside of a cup, round and around until it dies. Maybe you have spent years training yourself not to succeed and therefore have never had a success past a certain level. You now will have the know-how to break that cycle. Know that you've got it, believe that you've got it and go for it.

If you have lived and worked in the United States, you know it can be a very exciting place because it attempts to encourage free thought, and this type of environment is most conducive to heightened productivity. If you allow yourself to be left behind, you deprive all of us.

In the next section, we really begin dealing with the shenanigans of the concept development game. I'll give you the best idea possible about what to expect, but life is always full of surprises. Just remember to keep moving forward.

If you are still having trouble, consider the following:

Bounce-Back System

Sometimes we all just run out of steam without really understanding why, and then our concept or dream begins to wither. If you ever find yourself with those feelings, refer to these primer points:

1) Forgive yourself for any mistakes you made or commitments you couldn't keep. Learn and seek to move ahead to the best of your abilities.

2) Believe in your own talents and capabilities.

3) Recall that in the past there were certain goals you thought you had to have but didn't really need. Maintain a strong vision, but a realistic one as well.

4) When it comes to sales, don't finesse, impress. Customers will make their own choices, no matter what we want them to do.

5) In time, you'll always view the time you spent feeling discouraged to have been a waste of time. Learn, heal and move ahead. Build from the old to create the new. That is nature's way.

6) Don't allow yourself to be paralyzed by envy or anger at some other high achiever. These emotions are really a wish that the challenge was easier than it really is at the present moment. Use logic to tame negative emotions so you may share your best with the world.

7) Act or be acted upon. Inaction is a choice to deal with issues through weakness instead of motivation.

8) Those who don't have the good sense to recognize your potential do not deserve to profit from your ideas. Learn from them and move on.

9) Work with the possible and remember that you can always create new possibilities.

And now back to our main feature…

Moving ahead with Interest

Some of the respondents to your P.R. may be from some of the contacts you made in your initial research phase. That can prove to be a very encouraging development.

Last time you encountered these experts, you were just a babe in the woods, and they were the authorities. If you did your homework properly, the tables have now turned. Your efforts have elevated your value to your potential associates.

Hear these prospects out, but make no promises. Ideally, you'll want to entertain many possibilities before creating any type of written agreement. We're going to present a host of your basic options, and then you can decide what best suits you. Whatever you do, sign nothing, agree to nothing until a competent attorney reviews any and all proposals.

Some of you honestly feel that you have gone as far as you can on development and production planning. The nature of your product requires a specific manufacturing technology to move ahead. It may indeed be the correct time to explore potential associates.

If this is the right time to approach the heavies, let's do it right. We want you to be well protected. Arrange a meeting with the company's decision-maker(s) so you won't have to duplicate efforts or waste time with a go-between who could distort the hard information.

Be very open. Find out exactly what they want to do with your product and what they are willing to offer you. Remember, you are never to sell out completely. After all, as an expert on your product, your services could be of great value to them. If your prospects are smart, they will realize that they need you as much as your creation.

"Aren't I Supposed to Be Risking Something?"

You-Can-Do-It seminar coaches will all say about the same thing, "There's no opportunity for reward without risk." That phraseology is very deceptive for the vast majority of our readers and clientele. It's easy for someone else to encourage you to risk *your* money, but we think you can always afford to be careful. In fact, you *must not* jump ahead or risk heavy capital until your actual orders can support that risk and even then, study the alternatives, spread the risk and reduce the risk!

A Piece of the Pie - What, When & How to Give

What do you give an individual, company or investor who offers their services or finances in exchange for a potential piece of the profits of your company? While this depends upon a number of factors, there are some hard and fast rules to consider:

1) **Don't give away long-term interest for short-term favors**
If someone's doing a small money job for you, try to arrange liberal payment terms, if possible for the amount they are owed, plus agreed-upon interest. If you absolutely believe you have no other option, then get as much from this supplier as you possibly can.

2) **Don't make promises you can't keep**
Liability and accountability are increasingly used legal buzz words as production and service suppliers lose more sense of social responsibility. So while you want to wax enthusiastic about your concept when presenting it to others, don't promise untold riches! Always let the prospects draw those conclusions *themselves* from your presentation, but never make large financial rewards the reason for inviting participation. Remember, relevancy should come first.

3) **Insist upon 'maximum flexibility'**
If you have been told to make a plan and then stick to it, you are hearing incorrect information. The 'Connection' exercises of this book will be your marketing plan, and it will change and adapt as often as needed to meet your production and sales needs. Plan to be flexible, and insist upon the same behavior from your participants. Be crystal clear that your venture is a risk and may not yield any money for several months, years, or possibly never at all. If you encounter or discover you are dealing with an inflexible, demanding type, either let them know what the rules are in writing or plan to phase them out. Impatience pushes good ideas into failure.

4) **Non-lawsuit clause**
If you require your participants to sign just one document, make it a mutual written promise that no one may sue anyone else involved in the venture for any reason. Moreover, should a dispute arise, a mutually agreed upon arbiter shall be appointed to resolve any and all disputes and claims.

5) **Advanced buyout agreement**
Participants should know and agree *in advance* to appropriate terms for dissolution should the need arise.

6) **Performance agreement**
All promised dividends, etc., should be paid and/or delivered based upon supplier's delivery of results or earnest intent to deliver same. As long as best efforts are made to perform, the agreement is valid and dividends should be paid.

7) **The incompetence factor**
Should it turn out that a vendor, participant or supplier has misrepresented his or her talents and was never ready to deliver as promised, a proviso should enable the concept originator to render any agreement with said individual null and void.

8) **Stop at '51'**
Unless you and your associates (shareholders, investors, co-venturers, etc.) are offered a sizable **cash** advance for a majority of your company, always retain over 51% of your company, and always maintain personal veto power. There can be majority opinions against you, but you should always have the final say.

9) ***Net* not gross**
Your company could be taking in a great deal of money (gross profit), but after all expenses, including taxes, are deducted, there may be no actual remaining cash (net profit). Only offer payouts from net profit.

10) **Start at '5'**
Offer your long-term, permanent players a starting net payout of 5% once such net is realized. Also offer certain participants an opportunity to increase their profits providing they increase sales in some fashion.

11) **Don't be too generous**
While the success of your venture may hinge upon assembling the appropriate team, test your team first. Make sure you're working with the right players and be sure each is making best use of their respective gifts.

Inform your prospects that you feel it would be to their benefit if you stayed with the project through all stages. After you finish this book, you will find that you really can be of great value to them in many key areas.

You may consider suggesting to these serious prospects that your compensation be in the form of a modest monthly consulting fee plus a percentage of the gross profits that your product generates. This type of option can prove highly appealing to a company that originally thought they were going to have to pay you a small fortune up front. The way we have suggested represents a better risk for all parties concerned.

A business deal is not a good one unless it benefits all participants involved. Some of you may indeed require the services of a major distributor but may not need the manufacturing end. Consider the following:

Several years ago, I did the advertising for several pool and spa product companies. They made all the pool fittings, drains, skimmers, etc. One day as a favor to the boss, I made a delivery of prototypes to an injection-molding company. When I got there, I couldn't believe what I saw. It was my first time visiting a plastic molder. Here lie the deepest darkest secrets of virtually all the major competitors. This is where virtually all these different companies had their plastic pool components made, all by this one little company.

How could one company claim to be more special than the next? Anyone could stroll into that plastics company and have their product made and "Bingo" they're in business. It was really almost that simple, and I actually know people who broke off from a parent pool company and began their own successful enterprise this way. Of course, I should also add that they used our marketing techniques to really get an edge.

Don't worry, you'll learn all about our special promotional techniques in the upcoming chapters. Our only point with the great pool product caper is that you should not rush to give your product and profits to a big company who might end up using the same manufacturing company you would use.

Suppose you're planning to start up a small hometown paper. You could go to a local publisher who could essentially take it over. Or you could find a printer with periodical printing experience. No matter what you've got, if you attempt to line up your "jobbers," you can reduce your dependency on any type of parent operation.

Safety, Safety, Safety...

In pre-production, aside from protection, there is one other key element that cannot be ignored or overlooked. A lot of inventors are very rebellious, and then there are many of you who are strict conformists. The nature of your concepts could be as different as night and day, but in the area of state and/or federal regulations, safety standards or any other mandatory codes or laws regarding safety and approval of your goods or service, there are no shortcuts. If you think you know one, forget it.

Safety standards and the like are in place to protect all of us. Adhere to them like Krazy Glue. Determine if you need certain safety and/or other approvals and take proper steps to get them.

Have you ever bought a new screwdriver at a flea market only to find that it chipped away after its first use? What if a fragment caught in your eye? What kind of bargain is that? There are millions of such stories with much worse consequences. A bargain is a quality item at a lower price, not a substandard product that looks like a steal.

If you're out to make a quick buck and you have any intention of taking safety shortcuts, don't. You pose a real danger to the safety of all of us that you deceive into buying your product. Enough said.

Money Falling from the Sky?

As a result of your P.R. campaign, money may seem to fall from the sky. Some of you have been approached by people who want to help fund your efforts. These types fall into two basic categories:

1) The first is one who will give you a sizable amount of capital, essentially as a loan secured by your product. That kind of offer can tempt a lot of us, but it may be plain foolish to take on a loan burden at this stage of the game.

2) You could also be approached by the venture capitalist. This person may advance you a certain amount of money for the development of your product. You will pay him back by pledging to this person a modest percentage of your net profits for a specific amount of time.

Our rule of thumb for money offers is—don't take it unless you legitimately need it for your venture.

Two times in my life, I actually turned down venture capital. Once at age 23,

I had a small folk record company called "Warped Records & Tapes, Inc." I had invested twelve hundred dollars into this venture. After production of our second record, I was offered fifty thousand dollars in exchange for half interest in my company by a major stockbroker. Maybe I was overwhelmed, maybe I didn't believe it could happen to me. I turned the money down and Warped Records maintained its "nonprofit" status.

Another time I was offered seventy-five thousand dollars from a client of mine. He said the money was mine to play with if I could just present to him an idea good enough to invest the money in. I was so stunned—me, the guy who was always creative, suddenly was without a thought in my head. I couldn't think of anything and he subsequently invested the money elsewhere.

Money, by itself, at the wrong time doesn't always spell opportunity. Unfortunately, I wasn't ready for these two great opportunities, but both of these people are still very good friends of mine. Imagine what would have happened if I had taken the money with no real plan in mind.

Don't worry. There are many other times when I did utilize such money sources, but with a solid plan behind me. I've always preferred to keep my friends instead of trying to take the money and run.

Even with the absolute best of intentions, you are going to run into situations that may shock your sensibilities to the core. Broken promises, broken contracts, snake oil—the lessons come hard and fast. As long as you keep your sense of humor, you can persist and prevail.

Each chapter has represented specific missions for you to focus upon and achieve. You've come this far so you know your idea is a feasible one. A wonderful elderly Mexican friend always used to say, "Poco a poco, caminos lejos." Translation: "Little by little, we walk far."

So keep walking and protect yourself by protecting your interest in your creation. Economically successful nations are built on productivity, and productivity makes money, not the other way around.

2) Present Your Prototype to the Market

You have now gotten your product to the genuine pre-production stage. You have either married a company, or you have ventured out on your own. In either case, we have just barely begun to make things happen. Something you created or some concept you introduced is ready to happen on a level where it could prove profitable. You're excited, and you're already picking out the color of your Rolls Royce. Or your associated company, usually small, is hopeful that your product is going to work out.

What do you do? Do you make thousands of 'em? Millions? "Why not!" you think. Everything's ready to go. You and/or your developers have worked all the bugs out, and everyone seems to be suggesting "Full Speed Ahead."

Even if that's what your manufacturing associates or whoever are suggesting, present them with this premise and option.

☞ **Premise:** All parties with a vested interest want your idea to bear fruit as soon as possible so that a healthy road to profit can be realized. Of course! Well if your associates agree with this premise then you should propose the following option.

✎ **Option:** In that no one wants the road to profit interrupted once full-fledged sales begin, you need to do one final test.

Your associates may be somewhat annoyed at your insolence and suggestion of any delay at this point. You've already run a P.R. reaction test. You and maybe some technicians have tried to anticipate each and every pitfall.

You never know how your users are really going to react once they start using your product. Up to now, all of our tests and theories are only models that may anticipate what consumer reaction will be, even if some consumers have told you they know the idea is going to be a hit.

Will they say the same thing after they've actually used and worked with your product? No guarantees. One final test may save you a lot of problems down the road. If we are representing a new product, we attempt to give away twenty to one hundred of the product before releasing it for actual sale. With high-tech products, your budget may limit you from doing this. Even if you can get a few out in a good public field test, the benefits could save you a small fortune down the road.

Some pre-market tests involve thousands of giveaways or test-sales in various geographical areas. The majority of you will not need to go through such extremes.

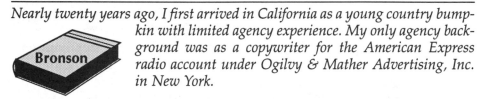

Nearly twenty years ago, I first arrived in California as a young country bumpkin with limited agency experience. My only agency background was as a copywriter for the American Express radio account under Ogilvy & Mather Advertising, Inc. in New York.

Once in California, with my reasonable degree of courage and some intelligence, I was destined to glean a very rapid education.

In L.A., my first boss was a very nice person who dressed well and meant well, but had not one inkling about how to create an ad. On my very first day, I was presented with an immediate problem. My new agency could not figure out why a certain account was so displeased with them. They had expended a lot of energy on the client's product, one of the first remote switches.

I was shown a magazine ad which they said produced no results. One glance at the ad and I was ready to wow them with my great advertising abilities. The ad displayed a gorgeous color photo with two people in their backyard spa, below which was a headline which read as follows:

". . . Presenting the Ultimate In Convenience"

Just what the public was looking for, the ultimate INCONVENIENCE. What an embarrassment. When they told me the ad was already in print, I would have quit that first day if I wasn't starving to death.

Find Out Before You're in too Deep

The time to make your mistakes is backstage, i.e. our testing phases. Relatively private screw-ups are nothing compared to the same hunk of stupidity times a thousand or a million. Protect yourself. And take chances? Absolutely. You gain nothing if you take no chances, but concurrently, you'll make no progress if you don't protect each step.

You've heard the expression, "Worst Case Scenario." What if wayward finances turn your best friend into your worst enemy? What if you're sloppy about the testing phases? Who's liable? You? Your affiliates? Plan and aim for success, but don't let your anxieties stop you from protecting yourself. And keep up that friendly relationship with your attorney. You can haggle most of the details, but your attorney can often very quickly insure that you made the agreement you thought you made.

Building good solid business friends can make a real difference. If your concept doesn't quite work out as planned the first time, don't write off some of your original associates. If they like the way you have presented yourself and your ideas they may well be apt to try it again with you.

After all, who is going to know more about what steps not to take than you? So let's see how well you can observe, anticipate and correct mistakes. Give your product or service to some average users for no charge, if possible. Let them play with it and run it through the mill for a few weeks, or longer, if necessary.

Encourage your subjects to be ruthless and excessive, but not dangerous. Then go back to them and beg for their worst, meanest criticism of your product. If they love it and have nothing rotten to say, persist until they come up with something good and negative.

Make certain you are in the proper frame of mind. Listen carefully to what your test market has to say. Write or record this feedback, and thank your subjects. Do not argue with them. Even though your concept may be very dear to you, just throw your pride out the window for now. Then go home and decipher the valid from the far-fetched. If you evaluate your data correctly, your pride will prevail in the end. If necessary, retrieve all of your products and bring them back to the drawing board.

If you had a hundred random test subjects and their responses were generally and genuinely favorable, that can be interpreted as a very healthy sign. If some of your subjects almost fight you and refuse to give it back, that's an even better sign, as you'll see in the next chapter.

If you got a lot of tomatoes in your face, fine. Go back and patiently make those changes. Then take a moment to thank your lucky stars that you have saved all interested parties from a devastating recall or worse. If ever you could tastefully recite the phrase, "An ounce of prevention is worth a pound of cure," and sound convincing, this has to be that time.

Don't Rush

You may not be ready to present your idea, which is perfectly fine at this stage. But for those who are ready for their first phase of presentation to your prospects, the time is right.

3) Create Inexpensive Resources

"Let's see. Do I want to spend thousands of dollars or hundreds of dollars (or even less) to achieve the same result?"

Of course you want to spend as little as possible to achieve a quality result. Your job is to convince your buyer of your professionalism. And if you can make an perfect-prototype that will impress and convince your prospect, isn't that the wisest way to go?

We've seen it all, or maybe we should say, we've seen them both—the big money deals and the small money deals. We've seen plastic mixing cup sets designed and engineered (including molds made) for over $150,000 (yes, that is a ridiculous amount of money). We have seen a similar competitive set made for almost no money. What's true here, as in most situations in our lives, is that some people buy more wisely than others.

In the following chart, our first subject could have developed that same concept for as little money as was spent by our second subject. Don't be alarmed by the extreme cost differences. We've been around a long time and that's why we've been able to come up with examples like this one. What the chart reflects are, in our experience, the absolute *best and least expensive* and the absolute *worst and most expensive* ways to put a product or service together.

Which Way Do You Want to Do It?

Item	Subject A	Subject B
Item	3-part drink-mix system	3-part drink-mix system
Prototype (model) Made?	Yes	Yes
Prototype Made From?	Clay	Scrap plastic
Is Prototype Functional?	No	Yes
Cost of Prototype	$2,500	Under $100
Was prototype presented to prospects?	No	Yes
If yes, to whom was it shown?	Not Applicable	Friends, relevant professionals, buyers, magazines (press releases), etc.
Were critiques evaluated before going into final manufacturing?	No	Yes
FINAL MANUFACTURING		
Materials	ABS Plastic	ABS Plastic
Design Cost	$10,000	Under $100
Engineering Costs	$140,000 to make mold, tool & die	Under $500
Most Work Done By	Outside professionals	Inventor/owner(s)
Inventor's experience relative to the idea?	None	Apprentice draftsman for an injection-molding company
PRODUCTION		
Quantity of initial production?	5,000 units	300 units (after '10' test)
Cost for initial run?	$8,000 or $1.60/unit	$1,200 or $4.00/unit
Feedback from initial distribution trials:	Negative—parts don't fit together properly	Positive, with minor adjustments required
Results	Must scrap most of first run. Loss in excess of $150,000 in first year.	Purchase order received. Credit given by mfg. for run of large quantity of units. Profit realized within first eight months.
Total Investment	$160,500	Under $1,900

You may very well not be able to put together all the resources required to do as well as Subject B, but hopefully you'll learn how to get as close as possible.

Though the above contrasts seem hard to believe, these stories happen all the time. Why is it that some people work wisely into profit while others merely spend themselves into discouragement? Which are you...perhaps a little of both? Well, that's why you bought this book. Are you getting your hands dirty or are you paying to watch from behind the front lines. Are your labors, value or talents somehow contributing to the profit or loss of your venture? Are you shopping around, comparing costs, looking for team players or co-venturers?

Aim to think and work like Subject B because that's how everyday people create opportunities for themselves; *by truly becoming an integral part of their idea, while teaming up when necessary with appropriate players versus merely contracting with various vendors.*

How to Be a 'B' from A To Z

We already know how Subject A thinks. He believes you need to spend your way to success. He either has a lot of money or has raised a great deal and is simply buying whatever he thinks he needs. Subject A figures, why analyze a problem when you can purchase a solution?

Whoever thought having too little money could be an asset? Not people who starve, or who have to sleep in their offices and skip meals to make ends meet. But there's one thing a poor entrepreneur/creator/dreamer does have, and that's the no-money option. Subject B had to approach every step as if he had no money for one simple reason...*he had no money.* Buying a solution was just not an option. But he did have determination, creativity, some applicable talent and a little space in his dirty little garage.

Now of course each situation is different. Maybe you do have a lot of money. It doesn't matter. The lessons are still the same. Every time B had a challenge or problem, he would find a solution using everything he had, with the exception of money. Having no money compelled him to think and make maximum use of his creativity and resources. He was determined to earn his market share.

While B wanted to make a model, he did not have the money to hire a draftsperson or designer or anyone. But he did have some scraps of plastic, some glue, some sandpaper and a can of spray paint. And he also had the commitment to spend most evenings after work in his garage working on his model using whatever he could find. Not until many months and many inexpensive failures later, did his concept begin to work close to what he had envisioned. In lieu of money, he gave his labor, his time and his own resources.

Alternatives and Connecting Those Dots

Still, Subject B's approach was not and is not the only way to proceed. Some ideas can be presented merely as a drawing or, in the case of service ideas, a brief report. The key is structuring your concept so it captures the imagination of that right manufacturer, distributor, buyer or rep. Sometimes, that will require a long hard road, and sometimes the right conversation with the proper trusted prospect can get you well on your way. If your idea has some relevancy to your gifts or your developing gifts, don't kill it with bad financial decisions. Find a way. Know that your aim is a top-quality result, but *think* as if you have no money.

Here's where we learn the importance of 'starting small.' You don't rent an office right away when your living-room, garage or kitchen will suffice. And *you don't expand without demand*. All of this backdrop should be stimulating you to rethink any previous notions you held about building your model. I know from experience that a great many of you previously assumed that you simply *had* to hire someone to build a model or to consult on the beginning aspects of your concept. The following chart is designed to dispel those thoughts.

Creative, Money-Saving Alternatives
For Starting Your Concept

Traditional Method	Creative, Money-Saving Alternative(s)
1) Consult with various field experts.	After appropriate protection, *talk, talk, talk*—network with potential experts. See who might be interested.
2) Ask others what their interest might be.	*Dare* others to participate. Have a think-tank party, etc.
3) Raise money to fund venture.	Assemble *resources*—individuals who will invest their skills or labor in whole or part in exchange for a share of potential profit.

4) Hire a general staff.	Create a team of interested, talented experts.
5) Hire (and pay) a design/ engineering expert relevant to field.	Give expert a percentage of future possible earnings in lieu of fee.
	Co-op with appropriate students, professors, starving artists, etc.
6) Hire a designer or artist to create non-working model.	Become your own expert. Make initial model yourself.
7) Purchase fully-functional components and then assemble concept with hired expert.	Make non-functional model initially just to gauge response from prospects. Use any scrap materials and attempt as professional result as possible.
8) Hire various marketing and advertising experts to present concept to market.	Present model to prospects on your own.
	Visit a relevant seminar (but don't buy a booth if you're still just exploring). If your concept is consumer-ready and if it's a household item or service, see if a local hardware store of supermarket will let you set up a booth and then progress.

In sum, scraping together whatever inexpensive or free resources you can muster (including yourself) can teach you extremely valuable lessons about the merits of your idea. However, spending an uncontrolled amount of money on the model/test stage before gauging the reaction of various prospects can become a lesson so expensive it can cost you the hope of an idea. Even if you have spent too much on your product so far, now you know better and now you can better manage your budget.

Given the base from above, let's now consider some of the creative ways to put your venture together, understanding that we are only limited by our own temporary lack of knowledge. So let's explore some additional alternatives.

Inexpensive Alternatives for Mass-Producing Your Product or Launching Your Service

Problem	Opportunity
1) "I'm ready to manufacture. I've tested my model and built a perfect or near perfect prototype, but I don't have ten cents."	If you're not in a position to borrow money, have you tried offering a prospective manufacturer a percentage of your future earnings in exchange for manufacturing your product?
2) "I've been to a few manufacturers, etc., and none will take a risk or invest in my idea."	*Sell* first. If your product or service is far enough along to make a positive presentation, try to get some prospective distributors, wholesalers, etc., to write a P.O. (a purchase order or a letter of intent to purchase). Very often, manufacturers or banks will loan money or advance production using such documents as collateral.
	Make it yourself. Can you set up an assembly-line in your garage, kitchen or living room? Will family or friends pitch in to help get you started? Who owes you a favor?
3) "I have P.O.'s and/or letters of intent but still can't get any favorable terms from my manufacturers. They're not bankers. They want cash."	If you are certain of your orders, perhaps a vendor will work out a payment plan with post-dated checks from your company. Is it possible for you to do some part-time work for the vendors in exchange for production costs or favorable credit terms?

4. "I can't afford a big-bucks or even a small-bucks advertising budget. How am I going to sell if I can't advertise?

You *can* advertise. Even the most sizable of success stories often had to create inexpensive alternatives for reaching their prospects. In the upcoming chapter, *Credible, Mostly-Free Advertising That Works,* you'll learn a wide variety of systems for attaining maximum exposure on a nearly minimal budget.

5. "I've tried everything and I just can't find any buyers or manufacturers."

Maybe you haven't tried to network as much as you need to. Overnight success can take several months or sometimes several years. Were you forced to give up, or did you merely *choose* to? Or maybe there's something basically wrong with your concept and you're not listening to or evaluating constructive criticism properly.

Starting out as correctly as possible can make all the difference in the world. It is okay and quite natural to make mistakes but *do it small*— learn on a small scale when it's safe and cost-effective.

Creating a venture is always a risky business. Will the product work? Will you commit to selling it properly? Will people buy it? But the more you learn early in the game about your prospects and about extreme cost-management, the more you turn the probabilities of success in your favor.

Are Your Manufacturing Costs in Line?

The above charts should help you to be realistic about your market price, both retail and wholesale. Providing that you have projected a competitive market price, are you properly managing your costs? Remember that most manufacturing costs should decrease as production increases. Use the worksheet to help monitor and manage your costs.

Be aware of and adaptable to changes and needs in the marketplace. The key issue in production is that there are always alternatives for putting your concept together. Some people find their starting components in the local electronics store, hardware store or supermarket and some require far more sophisticated materials, but usually not right at the beginning.

Know Your Resources

As exemplified in the "Money-Savings Alternatives" chart, to merely look for money as a starting point is often more of a mistake than a plus. Money is not the only resource that can help you get to where you're going. Human resources are the key.

Be a good shopper and keep your production quantities modest, even if it might cost you a little more in the long run. You may still have to make changes to respond to the competition. Don't make what you can't sell.

Connection #8
Cost Management Worksheet

The following is a straight-forward process for determining the cost-to-profit ratio for making your product. What you want to figure out is how to make your product or how to efficiently deliver your service in such a way as to realize a net profit after retail or wholesale transaction.

PRODUCT: _____

MANUFACTURING COSTS: QUANTITY OR WEIGHT

Raw Materials: _____ Costs$ _____ Per ____

_____ Costs$ _____ Per _____

_____ Costs$ _____ Per _____

_____ Costs$ _____ Per _____

_____ Costs $_____ Per _____

_____ Costs $_____ Per _____

Components: _____ Costs $_____ Per _____

_____ Costs $_____ Per _____

_____ Costs $_____ Per _____

_____ Costs $_____ Per _____

_____ Costs $ _____Per _____

LABOR COSTS (If Applicable) $ _____

SHIPPING COSTS (Manufacturing process only, if applicable)

_____

_____

TOTAL COST FOR MANUFACTURING PRODUCT: $ _____

$ per Product

1. To make _____ (quantity) of my product, the total cost per product is: (transfer from bottom of Connection #8)	
Use one or both of the following lines, but calculate each separately:	
2. The retail cost of my product shall be approximately: (Fill in this line only if selling directly to retail.)	
3. The wholesale cost of my product shall be approximately: (If only selling wholesale, use following line.)	
4. If selling to a **wholesale** market, approximate net profit is determined by subtracting line 1 from line 3:	
5. If selling to a **retail** market, approximate net profit is determined by subtracting line 1 from line 2:	

Manufacturing Credit

If sales response grows and you have worked with just a few producers and made a solid effort to cover your bills, these manufacturers may now be gaining sufficient faith in your venture's future to extend some credit.

Credit is generally extended based upon the grantor's belief in the recipient's ability to repay. And growth can often signify that repayment capability.

Have you assembled the right team who can best bring your concept to market, and are you an integral and viable resource for your venture? Question each step, question each expense. The best ideas are creatively built by individuals and not merely bought into.

To reach this point for your product or service, you expended a lot of enthusiasm, a lot of time, and you have learned well enough to see your product become real. You are probably quite proud of yourself. But, I'm sorry to say, you have picked the wrong time to be proud you don't get to do that until you have delivered and been paid for your first order.

Letting the world know you're out there—available for the right price to improve or enhance their lives in some way—that's the big trick.

Copy and use the next two pages to assist you in managing your idea as it continues to grow.

Components and Vendors

Company _____ Phone _____

Address _____

Component_____

Credit and Payment Terms _____

_____

Current Status (include modifications from original agreement and reasons)

_____

_____

Company _____ Phone _____

Address _____

Component_____

Credit and Payment Terms _____

_____

Current Status (include modifications from original agreement and reasons)

_____

_____

Company _____ Phone _____

Address _____

Component_____

Credit and Payment Terms _____

_____

Current Status (include modifications from original agreement and reasons)

_____

_____

Human Resources

List all contributing team players and their respective skills. This log should also include all persons who are working, designing or even producing, not for a fee, but for a share of the company.

Name _____ Phone _____

Address _____

Contributing Talent _____

Percentage of Net Profit contingent upon performance and results _____

Current Status (list dates and action) _____

_____

Name _____ Phone _____

Address _____

Contributing Talent _____

Percentage of Net Profit contingent upon performance and results _____

Current Status (list dates and action) _____

_____

Name _____ Phone _____

Address _____

Contributing Talent _____

Percentage of Net Profit contingent upon performance and results _____

Current Status (list dates and action) _____

_____

_____

_____

_____

Summary

Many entrepreneurs have little trouble bringing their concept up to a clear developmental point, only to be stopped dead in their tracks as they gear towards the marketplace. This breakthrough chapter has a number of important concepts for helping to overcome those barriers, proving once again that success is not always measured by R&D dollars, but a creative willingness to find a way through. This chapter could save you one-hundred dollars or hundreds of thousands. Starting to get your money's worth?

1) Maximize Your Concept's Value

❑ Don't lose control of your product. If you sell or lease your idea, maintain a degree of participation in the marketing areas.
❑ If applicable, entertain offers from co-venturers.
    1) Aim to remain involved with each phase of your product's development and sale.
    2) Utilize only the services you need.
    3) Review 11 points in "A Piece of the Pie."
❑ If you "sell-out"
    1) Get a production commitment or the product returns to you.
    2) Get a GENEROUS sum of money.
❑ Complete Connection #7 - Describing Your Idea
    1) Be simple and clear in your product descriptions.
    2) Describe what it is and does (features) and how your improvements will benefit the user.
    3) Include no photos at this time.
❑ If necessary, review the "Bounce-Back System"
    ❑ Move forward. Find out what's paralyzing you and get around it.
    ❑ Don't let old patterns hold you back. Approach your venture as an adventure and not a fear.
    ❑ If it's holding you back, find a way to get around it. Sometimes the only way to alter negative behavior is to put all the deep analytical thinking aside and just alter the behavior!

2) Present Your Prototype to the Market

❑ Insist on a pre-production market test.
❑ Develop a feasible test-market.

3) Create Inexpensive Resources

❑ **B** creative concerning your expenses.
❑ Complete Connection #8 - Cost Management Worksheet.
❑ Keep track of your current and potential resources.

Potential Challenges and Solutions

Challenge: Can't find a manufacturer that you feel comfortable with.

Solution: Sometimes, you'll encounter some very ruthless but successful folk that you just can't bring yourself to trust no matter how much money they may promise you. Pass them by. In the long run, you'll find it more profitable to work with a better communicator.

If you must work with someone who you fear may neglect their commitments, try to anticipate the worst thing they might do regarding your idea. Have a lawyer draft up the proper protective agreement and then proceed with a polite but tight leash.

Challenge: Project is not suitable for field-test.

Solution: Virtually everything can be tested. Essentially, an idea is a theory and a theory is a model of something that may or may not work. Have you done everything possible to prove or ensure the success of your theory before you go into mass production?

Once people see their product or idea ready to assemble, over-anxiousness often takes over at a time when common sense and logic is needed most.

A small test can prevent a large failure. Be sure to create as many success indicators as possible. And LISTEN to your results. Why do you think the gathering of information is called the gathering of intelligence?

Challenge: Project seems too overwhelming and burdensome.

Solution: Everything is big when we look at the whole picture at one time, and new things can seem a bit scary at first. So, tackle the component issues piece by piece.

No one is asking you to attack it all at once. When you feel tired and frustrated, walk away from it all. Re-approach it later with a clear head and a refreshed attitude.

Sometimes people get too rigid and impose impossible goals and deadlines on themselves. That kind of activity is merely a clever way of "flunking" yourself out of and escaping from responsibility. Your project is an important part of you. Keep the faith and perspective.

Challenge: Can't write those initial news release paragraphs.

Solution: Call a local paper, newsletter or magazine and ask them to do a small news write-up on your venture. Adopt and modify that copy for your other releases.

Challenge: Losing confidence in moving forward.

Solution: A fear is defined as anything we *perceive* as a fear. One person's boogie-man is another person's angel. Your lack of confidence is robbing you of your chance to get ahead and become a more fulfilled human being. You may need to modify your idea into something more interesting and motivating. Reread Chapter 1 and see if your rebirth puts you in the same place.

If you can't inspire yourself and you're still really stuck, ask a friend for honest support. If you need more of a boost, sometimes a clergyman can help. If not, don't be at all ashamed or embarrassed to see a psychologist once or twice. Many of this country's greatest business people and leaders often use the services of a corporate or other type of psychologist. Everyone can face challenges of growing and coping.

Any counseling that will get you unstuck and keep your idea alive may also yield the fringe benefit of helping to make you a happier person. Your project in itself can serve as excellent therapy because it can help to validate your essence. Give it a chance. Find and develop your own special formula to move forward to each succeeding step.

Before You Continue...

❑ Have you collected as much productive data as possible?
❑ Have you increased you concept's value without giving away pieces of it?
❑ Have you maintained high standards of excellence?
❑ Have you explored viable production alternatives?

Chapter Seven

Initial Sales
"Hello Out There. What Do You Think?"

> "*Sometimes the two most beautiful words in the English language are 'check enclosed.'*"
>
> Dorothy Parker

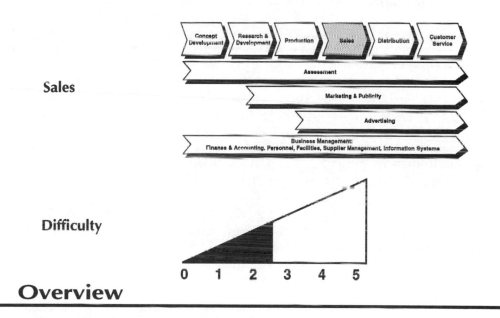

Sales

Difficulty

Overview

Ideas that give us growth and enlightenment are well and good, but when we convert these ideas into potential sales, now we're really connected. We now move on to building from feedback to refine your concept.

Action Steps

1) Create initial target linkage.
2) Turn respondents into sales.

1) Create Initial Target Linkage

It was frustrating in the beginning when we told you not to bother your friends at parties. You wanted to brag about this spectacular romance you were having with an idea.

Think back at what a shabby state your idea was in back then. What would your friends and associates have thought of you if that spark fizzled out? Now you are ready to profit from a little showing off. You've made it this far, and you're going all the way. It's time for them to bother you at the party.

Look Mom; I'm in the Paper!

We initiate our sales chain by taking that literary work of art you created in the previous chapter and getting it published. Call two local newspapers and tell them what you're up to—"Local Citizen Makes Good." Every paper has a space for that kind of material. Send them or, if possible, present in person your paragraphs about your widget, but NO PICTURES, PLEASE! Of you or especially of your product. All you're aiming to do with these P.R. announcements is to create curiosity. This valuable publicity should not cost you one red cent to run in your local papers.

There's no reason to worry whether your writing is good enough for the paper. If they need to, they'll perfect for you, free of charge. Then you'll have professional copy to adapt for future use.

Local Magazines

Plan these few releases in the papers at one-week intervals. Locate a local magazine and see if you can arrange publication of your release. If you know of a local trade magazine relevant to your idea then send your copy to them. Otherwise, just one or two local neighborhood or regional magazines will work just fine. We'll learn how to utilize those trade magazines in upcoming chapters.

Not every publication will accommodate your needs but many will. The magazine releases should appear about three to five weeks after your newspaper releases. That will give you more rewrite time, if needed. And remember, no pictures.

Radio and TV?

What about radio or TV? Is there a local radio station or two that your friends listen to? Radio stations have spots called P.S.A.'s (Public Service Announcements). If your product is in any way a community service, you can usually get a couple of these public service announcements read on the air for free. Try it.

I remember my very first radio interview. I was putting on a seminar and had  *sent out press releases to the local media. I really didn't know what to expect since this was the first time I had ever done anything like this.*

One afternoon as I was working at my desk, I received a call from a local radio station. The D.J. was the interviewer, and he asked if he could ask me some questions about my seminar while recording it. I was caught off guard because I didn't know that this was how people actually got on the radio, but I said sure.

He gave me a few pointers about how to respond to keep the interview going and then asked if I was ready? "Yes," I said, he began.

I remember feeling a little scared wondering if I was going to say the right thing and how was I going to sound on the radio, but it went fine. We finished, and the D.J. told me when it would be on the air. No problem! By simply giving myself a chance, I was able to speak to thousands of people.

Cable TV is giving the small towns a stronger voice with regards to local media happenings. I'm not asking you to put your face on TV yet, but a lot of these small town cable stations have TV bulletin boards. Get your announcement on TV if applicable.

Don't sit by the phone expecting miracles to happen. Some of you may get two responses. Some of you may get twenty. Be patient. This is feedback and refinement time.

2) Turn Respondents into Sales

Okay, you have gotten your initial P.R. going and your releases will all be appearing within the next month or two. You will be looking for just a small handful of credible responses. You should correspond or preferably meet face to face with at least five inquiries.

Why did they respond to your announcement? Find out what their specific interest might be in your gem. Build a file of each contact and their talents. Don't eliminate anyone as a possible participant at some future date unless they are dishonest or are simply trying to make money off of you.

All these people should be teaching you how to perfect your product. With every productive meeting your product should improve, as will your own value as an authority. It's a good thing you held out through this chapter because this is when the big business breakthroughs begin to happen.

Many of you will clearly see how to move ahead with all the energy in the world. Many of you will actually get offers of employment or capital to make your product go. Some of you will begin to create potential distribution avenues. This is a good time to court distributors and reps because they can give you an idea of how your product or service might best be shaped before you finalize it all.

If these releases don't catapult you into stardom, that's perfectly all right. The point is you have learned to develop a good idea without selling out or losing your shirt. Depending on your situation, you have saved anywhere from several hundred dollars to several thousand dollars.

A Second Round

After a few weeks or months, you may want to repeat this P.R. query process. To get a release in the exact same periodical, announce a new development in your work. Do not do more than two of these preliminary release programs because we want to get on to our production phase.

Party Time!

Now you can throw a party. Invite your friends as well as some of the new business contacts you made to celebrate the birth of your idea. The party should help create momentum and support. In a positive social environment where people are feeling their best, you'll get some very good advice and feedback. Just be dutiful about following up on the promises people make. That's your only way of finding out if the promises are real or not.

If your group is really feeling giving, give them some Post-its, have them write their ideas down (1 per Post-it) and stick them up on the wall. Create a competition to see who can get the most ideas up on the wall. When the flow of ideas slows, have the group move the ideas around on the wall to put similar ideas into groupings. When most of the movement has stopped, then have the group create several word titles for each grouping. As the party closes down, thank everyone for their input, and then get to work.

First-Timers Beware

Let the ideas flow. If your product requires any degree of assembly, you are looking for those components. For first-timers, we have two bits of advice about components.

1) Beware of the high cost of buying too cheaply. Why buy substandard or lower quality parts that could destroy your entire project, not to mention your business credibility? Components like that aren't a bargain at any price.

Whenever we trade stories with electronics marketers, we always seem to have a "new battery" story to laugh about. When first-timers have a product that requires pre-installation of household-type batteries, they almost invariably head across the border or overseas where they buy batteries for next to nothing. These foreign specials generally last just until the consumer gets the failed product. After all recalls for replacement with quality batteries plus repair of damage from their leaking predecessors, it's a bit difficult to view those cheap batteries as any kind of bargain.

2) So buy quality, and secondly make every effort to buy locally. If price is your problem here, negotiate. It's always better to keep it all local where you can have control.

If you're in the U.S., you've heard that your basic assembly labor costs are much lower overseas, but added to your overseas costs are the costs of shipping, insurance, etc. And international patent protection from such assembly plants is a real nightmare.

There are many able labor/assembly outlets throughout the U.S. whose owners want to work out a cost-effective arrangement. Give them a chance.

If your product requires simple assembly, why not consider the mentally retarded or other disabled or institutionalized people who could do an excellent job for similar costs? If your product is more sophisticated, explore various senior citizens or veterans organizations before you go trading overseas, and what about a local trade or business school?

Take advantage of your ingenuity before you rob your local economy of even a single job. You'll be more than just pleasantly surprised, your efforts could make you a community hero.

So for now, you have this wealth of knowledge and excitement that you have generated. How far you have come, yet don't be tempted to rest on a gratified ego. You can play those games after you succeed, otherwise you'll kill your progress.

You must organize all this data to give you fuel for progress. A danger point here is weak follow-up. Keep a planning calendar handy and be responsible about all your prospects.

Keep your development meetings to the point and don't let them stray. This is a time for good ideas and not for gambling. There's a great difference between activity and accomplishment. Think results.

Connection #9
Feedback—The Next Step

Use the logs on this and the following page to gauge responses from the newer, professional critics and consultants that you'll be dealing with, during this and especially the next chapter.

Professional People You Know

Name   Opinion

_____

_____

_____

Your Reaction _____

_____

_____

Name   Opinion

_____

_____

_____

Your Reaction _____

_____

_____

Initial Sales

Professionals and Relevant People Developed through All New Contacts, Press Releases, Networking, etc.

Name   Opinion

_____

_____

_____

Your Reaction _____

_____

_____

Name   Opinion

_____

_____

_____

Your Reaction _____

_____

_____

Name   Opinion

_____

_____

_____

Your Reaction _____

_____

_____

Power-Up Tip #5
Beating Burnout

> *"You can't always control what happens to you, but you can to some extent, control how you deal with it."*
>
> **Gordon Bronson**

At this point, you may be getting a little tired of your project. Putting any *Great Idea* into action requires full enthusiasm. You work relentlessly, striving for excellence. Time and ordinary routine succumb to the laser-like focus on the vision, causing the brain to be stuck in the 'on' position.

As you have by this time created a vision in which you truly believe, invariably you'll also reach certain points of mental hyper-drive, where your mind and creativity are functioning at an explosive pace. That's wonderful; that's often how great ideas become something even greater. However, as with everything in this life, for every intoxicating experience, there also exists the morning after—the creativity hangover.

Both of us are intense workers and players, and sometimes we don't listen to what our bodies are telling us because we become so enthusiastic about our work. As a result, we both have experienced serious bouts of adrenal exhaustion, and both have finally learned that you can indeed 'sprain your brain,' and get so involved in the vision that you become its prisoner instead of its beneficiary. Hence, part of reaching your vision entails appropriate pacing. Following are some important tips for preventing burnout and ensuring progress:

1) **Give It Your Best** - You want to make your project work and that means you have to give it your best. Identify your best attributes and contribute accordingly. Don't get bogged down in an area where you have no proficiency. You'll waste valuable time and increase frustration.

2) **"Can't we all just get along?" (No, not really)** - When building teams, you certainly want the finest human resources possible. It's also important to note that the whole idea of team entails mutual

cooperation. No venture is ever any better than the sum total of the personalities behind it. Make sure you have people around who:

- ☑ Will be responsible about their work.
- ☑ Will be good ego-free listeners and contributors
- ☑ Are neither greedy nor inflexible.
- ☑ Can manage anger and frustration in a mature manner.

3) Honor Your 'Cycle' - Even God rested on the seventh day. Work productively and efficiently, but don't merely labor without grander visions.

As with overeating, know when enough is enough, when you have done all you planned for that given day or week and when it's time to rest. Don't over-indulge in your own enthusiasm. Train yourself to rest with a clear mind no matter what happens that day.

4) Allow Things to Flow According to Chaos Theory - Many of the things we experience in daily life operate according to Chaos Theory principles, including our projects. Chaos Theory says that even in the midst of chaos is order. So, don't sweat it. If your project seems a little out of control, it will all come together in ways you can't foresee. We can also learn from Chaos Theory that the period directly preceding a breakthrough is often the most chaotic and frustrating. So, push on through until something manifests in your favor.

5) Keep Your Sense of Humor or Now is a Great Time to Get One if You've Never Had One

> *"The time to have confidence is when you absolutely don't deserve to."*
>
> Matt Doyle

Summary

1) Create Initial Target Linkage

- ❑ Submit your news releases for publication.
- ❑ Follow up with phone calls, when necessary.
- ❑ Seek out additional areas for media release, if applicable (radio and TV).

2) Turn Respondents into Sales

- ❑ Evaluate responses.
- ❑ Send out a second round of press releases.
- ❑ Throw a party and get some feedback.
- ❑ Determine how your respondents helped you to make a better product.
- ❑ If your product involves manufacturing and assembly, see if you can keep it local.
- ❑ Don't get burnout. Keep up the good work.

Potential Challenges and Solutions

Challenge: Fear of using the media.

Solution: Admittedly, it can seem like a scary prospect, but once you've first done it, it becomes easy and fun.

That local media is there to reflect news in your community. Your venture is news. Find the angle and spread the word to the best of your abilities.

Challenge: No responses to your media blitz.

Solution: It is extremely rare for no one to talk to you about your release. First, make sure your releases have been mailed, received and published.

Your release may be unclear, especially if this is your first venture. Did you get all the help you needed to get your message out in an understandable fashion? If readers are at all confused they'll pass it by.

Submit revised and corrected releases to the exact same publications. Explain what you think happened the first time around and ask for a second chance.

If everything checks out yet you still receive no responses, call some of your friends and pick their brains. Send clippings of your write-ups to potential manufacturers, distributors, etc., and follow up with phone calls.

Challenge: Everyone's saying it's impossible for the little guy to make it against the big guys.

Solution: We have books and successful careers that proves them wrong. Find the factors that will make your idea possible.

Impossible can often be a stupid word. There is always some way to address the issue. Ridiculous, however is a word you may want to listen to if you hear it a lot. If your venture is heading in the wrong direction, seek out the best advice you can muster, straighten it out and put those big guys in their place.

Be persistent with a good idea, but don't be stubborn about making a necessary change.

Challenge: Production and/or implementation seem too complicated.

Solution: Venders and suppliers want to make money. If you can work with them to develop a marketable product, their heightened interest will help keep the assembly phase alive.

Challenge: Can't put it together in the U.S.

Solution: You probably haven't shopped around enough. U.S. suppliers go bankrupt daily because they lack sufficient financial creativity to keep making their goods in this country.

How can you and a U.S. manufacturer team up to put your concept together in a cost-effective manner? Profit sharing? Other incentives?

Don't head overseas unless you've really exhausted all the possibilities, or unless yours is a task that might best benefit a developing country far more than the U.S. But be sensitive to the labor needs of your local business community.

Before You Continue...

❑ Have you made a real effort to coordinate and evaluate feedback?
❑ In development, are you solving the challenges by potential buyers?
❑ Are you building a workable team of cooperative resources?

Chapter Eight

Pricing, Sales and Distribution
Converting Dreams to Dollars

> *"The substance of any selling job is service."*
> **Anonymous**

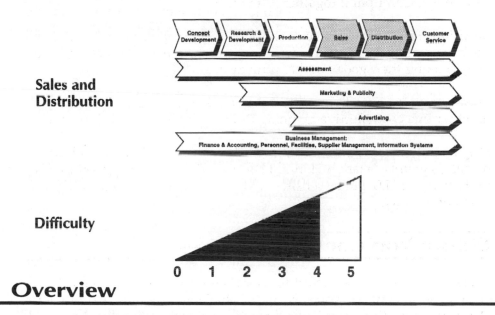

Sales and Distribution

Difficulty

Overview

If your idea is advancing appropriately, this becomes one of the turning-point chapters. Listen carefully to potential prospects. In roundabout ways, are any of them saying, "I might buy if you..."?

Action Steps

1) Transition from concept to commodity.
2) Get to market effectively.
3) Follow-up for success.

1) Transition from Concept to Commodity

For those of you with some sales background, this is an excellent period for you. You can finally ply your trade with more product knowledge and enthusiasm than you have ever had.

A lot of you, however, are chronic "sales how-to-aphobics." You're not only afraid of sales, you're twice as fearful about believing any advice regarding how you can become an able salesperson.

Pricing, sales and distribution are highly complex areas, and there are thousands of books dealing with these areas in particular. The only intention of this chapter is to make them relevant to your venture. Through this chapter, you'll get enough of a briefing to get things headed toward the results you need.

Much to your surprise, we are not going to cure you with a host of appropriate platitudes (though a few good ones come to mind). You can read every good authority and get a million good ideas. The real trick is to make it all relate to your venture.

Up until now, no book has ever proven to you that you can actually put all that good advice to work for you. If only one of these references could prove to you that you really can sell, then you would have the sufficient reinforcement to make sales happen.

Finally, you have invested in a book that's going to have you prove to yourself once and for all that you can sell, no matter what your background or fears.

It wasn't very difficult for most of you to engage those test subjects in the last two chapters. Did any of them really love your product or in fact express an interest in buying one? Very nice, you just made your first sale, and it didn't hurt much, did it?

Some of your test subjects have suggested refinements. Now that you have made those refinements, those subjects could also get very interested in your improved version. After all, you have improved life somehow with your idea. Everybody wants improvement in their day-to-day lives.

From the simplest, most direct and most important level of sales, person to person, your final testing phase has given you more sales experience than you ever realized. Your testers have worked hard for you and now they want to buy the perfected version. To show your gratitude for their help, you will sell it to them at a greatly discounted price.

Price! What about Price?

How do you know what to charge for your goodies? There are a few givens. In theory, merchandise must be competitively priced as perceived by the customer, but you also must make a profit.

Wait a minute! There are excellent pens for well under a dollar and there are pens priced at several hundred dollars. Therefore, competitive pricing also refers to the class and quality of the product.

Our ears ring daily from the barrage of special value sales that in essence suggest, "Get the same quality at a lower price. "

The following client wished to remain anonymous. You'll soon see why. After several years of a mutually profitable relationship, he informed me one day that he no longer needed my marketing and advertising services. He was a "slow-pay" client, so I was somewhat relieved at losing the account.

Three years later, a former associate of mine sent me a clipping. My old pal had gone bankrupt. Though I was certainly sorry to hear of his losses, I had to confess to an inward pleasure of seeing the consequences of the absence of my services.

I decided to call him to find out what happened. I knew his products were some of the finest on the market, but the competition was creeping in. Without any marketing expertise, all he knew how to do was lower his prices, which finally got so low, his business collapsed.

Quality wars are better than price wars. Your efforts thus far should permit you to be competitive if your product represents a realistic improvement. Price wars can cheapen the public's image of your product and then wipe you out.

There's a lot more involved in the pricing process than the mere comparison of a final selling (retail) price. Somehow, you have to eventually absorb all start-up and research costs. A competent tax accountant will help you to realize any legitimate deductions for your efforts, as well as all tax obligations.

After deductions, you must determine what your actual expenditures are. From inception to production, you can't miss a penny. And it doesn't stop there. What about shipping, distribution, and advertising? Who pays for it all?

Every step toward the final consumer shaves a little of your profit away. Still, there are ways to keep those costs down to a bare minimum. The adage of cutting out the middleman is more gimmickry than anything else. You may need legitimate middlemen to ensure that your product sells on a large scale.

There are many creative means to cover costs. For example, one fall I was putting on a seminar at my university for a student organization in which I was involved. I didn't have any money to pay for the event, so I decided to sell advertising in the event program to cover the costs of the event.

Local companies which would benefit from this focused exposure to their target market were glad to pay $75 to $250 dollars for advertising space in the event program. I was able to generate enough revenue from this advertising to completely cover the cost of the event.

It is also important to note that advertisers in the program were willing to pay for the value which they perceived they would derive from this advertising medium. The price they were willing to pay had nothing to do with how much effort I put into the project or how much it was going to cost to make the program.

So, when you consider what your price will be, make sure you focus on what the customer is willing to pay based on the value that you are bringing to the market.

We had previously suggested that you could consider controlling the manufacture of your idea. If you have done that, you can now potentially earn a bigger piece of the pie for your efforts. It is critical in pricing to be market-sensitive, competitive, quality/value oriented and never arrogant.

Instead of approaching a manufacturer, you could make a similar deal with a competent distributor, although there are excellent ways to begin as your own distributor, as you will soon see.

2) Get to Market Effectively

Unless born from a merger of two monster-companies, most businesses began as small mom and pop garage ventures. Distribution may have meant driving around in the old jalopy and dropping off the goods at a few households for a certain retail price which, for this example, we'll set at $5.00 per item.

A couple of local little stores wanted to buy the product. Our little manufacturer/distributor sells his product to them at the wholesale price of $2.50.

In time, hundreds of stores want to sell this product, far more than the jalopy can cover. Enter the distributor who buys each item for $2.00 and then distributes it to the stores for the wholesale cost of $2.50

How do you connect with all these distributors and retailers? That's one of the gems of sales success; locating the unlimited sales avenues to select the one that's right for you.

Trade Shows, Flea Markets and Fairs

If admission of ignorance is the first step towards wisdom, then I guess you'd have to say that brokering officially licensed products from the '84 Olympics made me and my associates very wise. Much of this account was a heavily intensified and rushed education about every aspect of product development and sales.

My favorite part of that entire period were the trade shows and conventions. That was where everyone really got the chance to ply their trade. The salespeople sold at their best, the buyers bought, often more than planned due to the excitement of it all, and ideas flutter back and forth like the swallows changing direction at Capistrano.

I had represented scores of products at many shows before the Olympics, but never such a diversity in such a short time. If you have never been to a convention, trade show or seminar in your field of endeavor, you're really missing something.

If feasible, try to introduce your product or service at (or at least attend) a relevant trade show, carnival, flea market or fair. These can all be excellent avenues for building your sales knowledge and confidence.

You can find so much valuable sales, pricing and distribution data during a day or two at the right event. Generally, all the heavies in your field will be there and you can see just where you and your product stand.

Of greater interest is that you could make some great sales at the right event. Two words of advice:
1) In all the excitement, you'll hear a lot of empty promises. Try to sort them out, then find and cash in on those few real leads.
2) With every interaction, collect a business card and on the back of that card note intentions with that prospect.

To make this financially feasible, we are looking for broadscale success. One show is just a speck in your overall sales plan.

Power-Up Tip #6
Internet Sales and Distribution

Given all of the publicity back in 1994 concerning doing business on the Information Superhighway, or Internet, we would be remiss if we didn't include information on this growing topic.

Need Information: Internet Proves that Genies Are Real!

Make a wish, any wish. What do you want for your life and your career? Who are the people and organizations you need to find to really rocket your venture to success? This book explores all the ways to find them and one of the best, is also one of the newest—Internet. Some of the best lines leading to your success are "on-line."

That's right, that scary concept known as the Information Superhighway. To the millions of neophytes who must learn about internet and its cousins—Prodigy, Compuserve, America On-line, etc.— driving on the Information Superhighway has the feel and appeal of riding a bicycle against traffic on the L.A. freeway—sheer overwhelm.

In truth, after just a few hours of test-driving, the Internet 'net' can become your greatest ally in almost every area of your life. Imagine instant access on almost every topic you can dream of, and not just information, but interaction, bulletin boards, catalogs, associations, discussion groups; it's like being at one grand social gathering where you can choose and change the guest-list at will. Searches that used to take weeks, months or years, and lots of chance luck, have now become organized, categorized, focused and available to you in a fraction of the time, and very often, at almost no cost.

At any age, at any stage, with any concept, make a wish or two and then jump on the Internet. If you're truly dedicated to the success of your venture, you'll get on "the net."

See It as Accelerated Networking in the Real World - Internet Sales

Because the Internet evolved from a grass roots level, it has also developed a "culture" that is unique to its historical development. Where most people get in trouble advertising on the Internet is when they assume that it can be used to create and distribute "junk mail." Instead, picture Internet advertising as an extension of the personal, word-of-mouth advertising that you do all the time outside of cyberspace. If you treat people with respect on "the net," they will refer others to you.

There are some news groups which do allow open solicitations:

- aol.commerce.misc-ads

- biz.comp

- biz.comp.services

- biz.misc

Setting up Shop - Internet Store Fronts

With the proliferation of the World Wide Web on the Internet, many people are setting up their own store fronts or working through a "mall manager" to get a store front in a "mall." WWW allows consumers to "walk-in" to your "store" and look around through a graphically driven interface which can display pictures of your product. Moreover, WWW store fronts allow the customer to hyperlink into more detailed information on your products/services or additional related products/services.

"Malls" are popping up on a regular basis, so you need to do your homework if you decide to go this route. One "mall manager" we found can set you up with a basic store front for under $1,000 with multiple options that can add an additional $100 to several thousand to your bill. As is obvious, this is not necessarily an inexpensive alternative, but it may be just what your idea needs. But with all of the free network newsgroups, bulletin boards and message centers in the various on-line services, you may not need a mall service.

Additional electronic mall information can be found through:

Branch Information Services

☎ 313-741-4442

💻 info@branch.com

Global Network Navigator

☎ 800-998-9938

💻 info@gnn.com

More Information

More information on doing business on the internet can be found regularly in the Internet World magazine and in the following newsletters:

The Internet Business Journal

☎ 613-565-0982

💻 mstrange@fonorola

The Internet Letter

☎ 202-638-6020

💻 info@network.com

Internet Business Report

☎ 800-340-6485

💻 rob@ost.com

To keep up with the fast pace of change on the Internet, you may want to consider subscribing to "net-happenings." This on-line publication is produced multiple times daily and can be received in the full blown form or in a digest format. To subscribe, send message to:

💻 majordomo@is.internic.net

with a blank subject field and the following in the body of the message:

💻 subscribe net-happenings

or

 subscribe net-happenings digest

Back issues of these publications can be browsed via gopher and World Wide Web.

Good luck with your journey on the Information Superhighway!

Getting in the Game

Some of you are planning to open up a specialty retail store, or utilize flea markets, malls, direct-response radio or TV to sell your product directly to the public. Any of these means can be a good and sensible way to start if you can manage the capital appropriately. You may, however, want to first try out your wares in an already existing store, if feasible.

There are as many ways to get your goods or services to market as there are products. The key is finding where you and your concept best fit in the consumer/end-user arena. Throughout this book, we have explored the most cost-effective means to achieve our successes. Remember that almost anything can become a yes if you listen carefully enough as to why you got a no.

At this point, refer back to the last several pages of Chapter 5 and 'Connection #6, *The Yes Chart—A Simple, Systematic Approach for Closing a Sale*.' If you remember, this chart can assist you in getting past no to a YES!

Distribution and Sales

There is a great temptation to want to celebrate once a concept has been brought to reality before any actual sales are made. Yet too much excitement before a sales network and demand have been created will only yield to excessive impatience and disappointment. The best-made and best-priced product or service in the world still has to be properly distributed.

On the following page is a chart to hopefully either get your initial sales going or bolster existing sales.

All the Right Moves

The Wrong Way	The Right Way
1) Pay advance salaries to sales reps to have them attempt to sell your untested product/ service.	A qualified sales rep will not charge to present your concept to market providing your concept is of sufficient quality, relevancy, price and appeal. Reps should be paid commission standard to the trade. Could you be your own rep, either store-to-store or via distributors?
2) Rent your own store or office space before trying to determine or establish demand for product.	Maybe another retail establishment will allow you to use some of their space.
3) Concentrate on only one way of selling.	Modestly test as many sales avenues reaching your prospects as possible, e.g. retail store, mail-order, catalog premium offer.
4) Send out sales letters to the general public.	Send out a quality brochure, complete with mail-order response to a well-researched target audience.
5) Set a 'quota deadline,' after which time, you should give up if sales don't meet your expectations.	Any businessperson who wants to succeed knows that they have to sell and learn until the sale is made.
6) Use the telephone to network like crazy. Have long conversations to show how pleasant you are.	The phone can be anyone's most vital tool if you focus in on your market with polite, to-the-point conversations. You may want to prepare a calling script. If they're not interested, find out why and note in your response log.

Some of the Keys to Successful Selling Are:

1) **Self-Belief** - Yes, you've heard it in so many 'you-can-do-it' manuals, but sufficient belief in one's self simply can't be commanded. So try reason; if you have chosen your concept correctly, it should be something that is somehow a part of you and should then encourage you to represent yourself honestly with relaxed confidence. Some people complain that they are not salespeople, but in fact, we all have to represent ourselves to survive. Courage is a choice. Cowardice is a choice. And there will be no growth and no opportunity for financial gain without some self-belief.

2) **Don't draw conclusions for the prospect** - If you're doing your job correctly, your prospects will draw the appropriate conclusions. It is your task to explain the function of your concept and its specific features and benefits.

3) **The Truth** - Don't fool yourself by seeking to hear what you *want* to hear, as opposed to what you *need to hear*. As early as possible in the development of your concept, learn the truth about your product. What will you need to do to make your product saleable. The sooner you find out, the sooner your chances for success.

4) **Politeness vs. Charm** - Courtesy is always important no matter what you hear about your concept from prospects. Perhaps if you listen to them and evaluate their feedback properly, they might be your best customer one day.

5) **Don't push, don't beg!** You resent being forced into something. Your prospects are human too. If you try too hard to make a sale by begging for a trial, offering a ridiculously low price or by lying, your prospect is not going to have too much faith in your concept.

6) **However...**Don't let an opportunity pass you by. Sometimes you may try something that requires flexibility in order to get a sale rolling.

3) Follow-Up for Success

Follow-Up and Growth - Turning the Promise into Payment

It is one of the more gratifying experiences to have built up a concept to the point of sales. This can also be a time of great danger and frustration for a new business. You now know that your concept is viable. You have seen ever-growing and ever-promising test results, but then how do you bring it to the point where it becomes a viable, profit-making enterprise?

What most people learn about sales is that there is no limit to what they themselves can do, but on the other hand, anxious would-be entrepreneurs learn that nothing is an automatic process.

Even after you've completed your various test phases, you're still going to be testing. What did you do right that won the sale, and what did you do wrong that limited or prevented a sale? Successful follow-up is a willingness to learn, to evaluate, to admit mistakes and faults; then, you must convert those mistakes into profit-making lessons. Test yourself with the important follow-up rules to live by in the following "Connection" exercise.

Connection #10
The Follow-Up Challenge

If a prospect expresses interest, find out:

1) Prospect's needs
   - ❑ How used or resold?
   - ❑ What is their marketing program?
   - ❑ What modifications could you feasibly make to accommodate client?
   - ❑ Would these modifications serve other clients more effectively as well?
   - ❑ Would these modifications help you to diversify and create a new product?

2) Prospect's Sincerity - Attempt to either close (complete) a sale or send a proposal and then follow up within one week.
   - ❑ If prospect continues to call and seek free advice, set a limit. Get proposal out and set your fee.
   - ❑ Have you set up specific and mutually agreeable payment terms?
   - ❑ If renegotiation is necessary, get your money; do so but make sure you get paid.
   - ❑ If the goods were delivered and accepted in good faith, then it's your money that's owed to you.
   - ❑ Do not let receivables lag behind. Suspend further delivery of goods until account is rectified.

3) Your Approach
   - ❑ No matter the situation, have you handled it politely? Remember that today's headache could be tomorrow's bonanza.

The following "Connection" exercise is provided to help you monitor and develop sales progress all the way to a successful sale.

Connection #11
Chart Your Own Sales Success
(Check One)

❏ YES   ❏ MAYBE   ❏ NO

Date _____ Business _____

Name _____

Contact _____ Phone _____

Best time to call _____

Address _____

Response to your concept: _____

_____

_____

_____

The prospect would buy if you:_____

_____

_____

NO - If prospect is not going to be viable, check 'no' at top of page and then use a new page for another target.

MAYBE - If future sale is possible, check 'maybe' at top of page and save this and the next page for continued sales tracking of this prospect until a definitive response is achieved.

YES - If a successful sale is made, check 'yes' at top of page and fill in the next page.

Payment Terms

Sold To: _____ Address _____

_____

_____

Amount Sold: _____

List Purchase Order Number: _____

Ship by: _____

_____

❑ How do you know if you'll get paid?
❑ Can you ship C.O.D.?
❑ Can you ask for even a partial down-payment?
❑ What are your liabilities?

Do not ship until you have worked out mutually agreeable payment terms.

List terms: _____

_____

_____

_____

_____

_____

_____

_____

_____

_____

Summary

1) Transition from Concept to Commodity

❏ Establish fair and competitive pricing.
❏ Try to avoid using price as the main selling point.
❏ Emphasize quality of goods or services.

2) Get to Market Effectively

❏ Go back and sell your product to your test market. Offer these individuals a generously reduced rate.
❏ Determine most appropriate distribution avenues.
  ❏ Talk to major retailers.
  ❏ Talk to distributors relevant to your market.
  ❏ Try trade shows, flea markets and fairs.
  ❏ Check out the Information Superhighway.
❏ Review "All the Right Moves" in this chapter to brush up on your selling techniques.

3) Follow-Up for Success

❏ Use Connection #10 for every prospect which shows interest.
❏ Use Connection #11 to keep track of your prospects and ensure that you will get paid.

Potential Challenges and Solutions

Challenge: No confidence in selling your concept.

Solution: You have defined your goals and now must become comfortable with your project. You must believe in what you're doing, or no one else will.

Be flexible and don't expect to make every sale you attempt. Learn from each prospect so as to increase your chances for success with your next prospect. Some of your best experiences will emanate from your sales experiences as you discover first hand what distributors and/or the general public will and will not buy from you.

Challenge: Can't come up with a competitive price.

Solution: Some products or services command higher prices than others in a similar category. Price can be measured by what a willing buyer will pay to a willing seller. If you have a superior concept, price won't be the major issue.

If your product is similar to existing ones, except yours costs more, why should people pay more for almost the exact same thing? Take a careful look at your competition and determine what features you could create to stand out and thereby merit a higher price tag.

Re-examine your manufacturing and distributing costs. These entities don't want to overprice themselves out of business. If necessary, get them to bend at least for the first six months of production.

Challenge: Can't find a distributor.

Solution: All goods are distributed somehow. A call to a couple of disinterested distributors means nothing. There are thousands of distributors and an equal number of creative distribution options.

You have to attract, persist and sell them at a price that must guarantee a profit for yourself. Consider all cost factors carefully.

Your first ad campaign can create a number of options that could build some sales volume, after which time you could be in a stronger position to approach a distributor.

Before You Continue...

❑ Have you developed a sense of pricing or general worth of your concept that is all market and no ego?
❑ Are you developing commitments that advance or imprison you?

Chapter Nine

CREDIBLE, MOSTLY-FREE
ADVERTISING THAT WORKS
"Hey Boss, Look at This."

> *"The world cannot welcome you if they do not know you exist."*
>
> Howard Bronson

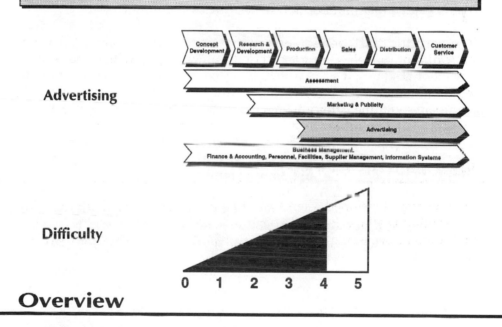

Advertising

Difficulty

0 1 2 3 4 5

Overview

In advertising, you can get a lot of reassurances. Unfortunately, they're generally from advertising salespeople. There are no promises from maximum exposure, so in this chapter, we offer you maximum insight to minimize risk.

Action Steps

1) Understand how advertising really works.
2) Identify media targets.
3) Create a professional image.
4) Get your message placed.
5) Focus on your audience.

1) Understand How Advertising Really Works

Advertising—Madison Avenue; those creative geniuses who have the power to make you buy or do anything.

There seems to be a buyer (market) for everything and anything. All you have to do is find it and influence it. We are told that obnoxious, repetitive TV commercials actually make us remember to buy those products. Are we really all that stupid or is what we generally see as advertising simply the best we are capable of?

As advertising and consulting professionals (or persons, depending on your point of view), we watch the TV commercials more than we watch conventional shows. It's like watching twelve little shows every half hour. Commercials seem to be getting more glitzy and creative all the time. But is the increasingly shrewd consumer really buying all this new vaudeville?

Are we looking for reflections of trends? Not especially. Technique? Very often. Do we believe the claims we see? Very rarely. In fact, the TV is our lantern looking for an honest commercial.

Credibility—that's what you're after. How can you ever really be sure that people who buy their own commercials are telling you the unbiased truth? Some present what they call hard facts and statistics only to be rebutted by a competitor's contradictory facts.

Very often, paid ads lie, and that seems to be acceptable because people have traditionally responded by purchasing those goods or services.

So where do we find our trends? We watch and read the news, everything we can get our hands on. We don't believe what people or ads tell us unless we can really prove it. Try this: Go out and buy one of our favorite magazines, *Consumer Reports*. Pick out a couple of products that you believe to be the best available, and then see what *Consumer Reports* has to say about it. Generally, you'll be surprised and disappointed.

The Credibility Factor

When they advertise, you need to scrutinize. "Deeze Dem Doze" clients would throw me a chunk of money, as if it were a dog bone and say, "Buy me an ad in dis here magazine." (Generally referring to the magazine of their trade.) I made a healthy profit, and they would see themselves in the magazine. The only problem was I wasn't giving them the sales they needed.

Bronson

If an advertising agency has already tried to get their hooks into you, they have most likely told you that paid advertising is the only way to succeed. Since selling and producing ads is probably the only way they can stay in business, what on earth else are they going to tell you?

Well now you know differently. First of all, you have a leg up on most ad agencies because of the mountains of research you have already carried out. Research and homework are where any real advertising campaign actually begins. Ironically enough, it is often the weakest area for agencies. They'll give you a ton of ideas on how to spend your money, but not much actual research. That's why our "Deeze Dem Doze" clients get so mad. They spend a wad of money on a couple of ads against our recommendations, and then they tell us advertising doesn't work.

Just because a salesman tells you to buy an ad doesn't mean that you just bought a ticket to guaranteed success. Challenge those salesmen. How many of them would only take a fee only if their ads worked? Witness credibility succumbing to mere greed.

When we're given a budget to make a product successful, we consider that money to be a loan that we aim to pay back tenfold. We spend very little of our client's money until we can make that client's business grow. A no-response ad campaign does more than make a client mad, it's a dream-killer, and we have promised to protect your dreams.

Put those advertising agency and salespeople on hold for now. Don't join the hundreds of thousands of people who waste billions on incorrect advertising procedures. If the masses want to keep wasting their money, that's their problem.

2) Identify Media Targets

The World is Not Divided by Geography, but by Multimedia

For your debut, we have a far more credible procedure that will cost you next to nothing. Most of you are more than halfway there already. We have often asked audiences to guess how many magazines are printed in the world today. We hear numbers like a hundred or a few thousand, but never the actual number which easily exceeds several hundred thousand. Name a topic, any topic whatsoever. There's a magazine that covers that subject. Ever heard of *Ballet News,* or *Bow and Arrow Monthly,* or *Totally Housewares?* How about *Poultry Digest Magazine* or *Plastics Business Magazine?*

The world is not divided by countries, cities or towns, but by thousands of subcultures represented both by publications and the ever burgeoning information superhighway, a.k.a. Internet. Each month, over thirty thousand people read *Ballet News.* Over one hundred thousand read *Bow and Arrow* each month. Any topic, no matter how bizarre or mundane, has a relevant magazine or newsletter and a world of people whose livelihood and or lifestyle is affected by it. Are you aware of the publications that pertain to your product? Here's how you find them.

Connection #12
Target Newspapers and Magazines

Your assignment is to track down ten publications in each of the three categories, if that many exist. For our purposes, the three categories of publications are:
1) Newspapers: local and national.
2) Consumer magazines, i.e. those geared to the public retail trade.
3) The mighty trade, technical and professional magazines targeted to product manufacturing, distribution and all other pre-consumer areas.

Newspapers

The newspapers should just be your everyday papers on a local and, if possible, national level.

Consumer Magazines

For the consumer magazines, if possible, at least five should be relevant to your product's industry.

The other five require a little brainstorming on your part. They should be general or broad topic magazines where an audience for your product or service may be available. For example, if you've invented a pair of scissors, you may pick up a hardware journal or cutlery news but you should also pick up a magazine about paper products, textiles or maybe school supplies. You're seeking out related industries.

Technical or Professional Magazines

Use the five and five rule for the trade technical or professional magazine category as well. Now, how do we know these publications exist and where the heck do you find them? The easiest place to start is at the manufacturers that you've dealt with. They'll generally have the trade magazines of your industry lying around somewhere.

If you can't hunt them down that way, there are some excellent reference books that list every publication you'll ever want to know about. If you know of a local ad agency, see if they will lend you these directory books for a few hours. If that is not possible, check your local library for any of the writer's market books.

Two of the prevalent directories are:

 Standard Rate and Data Service
(800) 851-7737

 Writer's Market
(800) 289-0963.

Some are expensive to buy, but their data books list everything ever published. Check your local library first for the software or the book.

For the publications you have picked, get copies of as many of them as possible. Take a few minutes to get familiar with each one. Especially in the trade mags, study the ads, some of which may one day be your competition.

How do manufacturers and distributors keep an eye on the competition? There are many sophisticated ways. One way is to stay well-read. Keeping an ongoing monitor on the market means all manufacturing costs and technological developments are up to date.

"Hey Boss, Look at This!"

You could watch or read ads, but you already know that ads aren't your most credible source of information. Let me tell you about a holiday that occurs at nearly every manufacturer or distributor just about every few weeks. It's called, "Hey boss, look-at-this" day.

On any given morning when the trade magazines arrive, the salespeople rush to grab a copy, of which there are generally several. Do they quickly skim through the ads? No. Do they sit down to read a nice long article? Not at this time.

You will see them turn to one place first and study it intently. That section is known as the "New Product," "Product News," "Industry News" or a number of other similar headings. Their eyes feverishly scan this section looking for what the industry is up to, studying the competition. The moment they see something that may affect their own product line, they dash into the main office and say, "Hey boss, look at this!"

After years of advertising and scores of accounts, we have seen more things happen from the New Product sections than any other area of advertising. Those who followed the procedure we've outlined in this chapter have loved the money we have saved for them while giving their product a chance to prove itself.

Everyone benefits from proper use of the media. That's what you're learning here. Your first big media lesson will be through the magic of these New Product sections. If you receive tremendous results from a particular magazine, that may be the place to go for future paid advertising. This initial campaign is not a P.R. tactic. Public relations involves using the media to showcase civic interests of an individual or organization. Proper public relations will play a very powerful role for your cause as you will see shortly.

For now, we are going to promote your concept on a very wide and powerful scale for almost no money and certainly a savings of several thousand dollars in advertising expense. We can do this because the cost to run a blurb and photo on your product is generally zero, free, no money.

Though some magazines do charge a space fee for their New Product sections, most do not. Those that do not charge a fee are the smart ones because they invite and encourage the growth and prosperity of the free enterprise system. They invest a pittance in giving this space and if that helps to make your product a success, it could pave the way for a mutually profitable relationship.

There's an even more significant reason that they should give you free press. The introduction of your product or service is news and it's their job to report the news. For a magazine to run one or two releases over a few months for you is usually no problem. Any more than that for the same new product is taking unfair advantage of the media system.

3) Create a Professional Image

Doing Business As...

Time to build your image and substance in the corporate world. To start, we would like you to go to your local budget printer and have some business letterhead put together. You should develop a simple logo from the printer's art books, and include your name, phone number and address.

Print one hundred envelopes, cards and letter stock. This whole process should cost between one and two hundred dollars. If you have become affiliated with a company, use their letterhead and have them print business cards with your name on them.

Another alternative to consider using is high quality, specialty papers and a good laser printer to build a complete business look at a fraction of the cost of a custom print job. This is a rapidly growing industry as many people are leaving the corporate world to strike out on their own. The down side to specialty papers is, in fact, their popularity. They have become so wide spread in use that now people can usually recognize specialty papers from custom designs. This may not be good for your enterprise, especially if you want to be remembered as being unique.

If you're stuck for a good name for your company, don't settle for anything sarcastic. Cute or clever names are fine as long as they clearly indicate what the business is all about and do not offend. Otherwise, use your last name followed by the publicly known name of your product. Example: "Jones Fertilizer Company" or "Smiths Laser Engineering."

If you need a title under your name and your item is a product, consider using the following label: "Product Research and Development." If your enterprise is service oriented, try "Manager" for blue collar or "Program Director" if it's white collar in nature.

If you think you can get away without using letterhead, remember you will already be saving several grand in advertising costs. From an established image and credibility standpoint, get that letterhead, even if you can only afford fifty pieces.

For Example...

To take the next steps for both my goods and service readers, we are going to create two fictional businesses. We'll call the first one "Women's Work, Inc." Two young women, one a single mother with no educational background and the other, a two-year business student with a knack for successfully starting small businesses, have formed a management company to help young women begin their own businesses.

We'll call our product company "Adams Reliable Auto Products" (Inc., if applicable). Retired chemist Fred Adams has developed a substance that not only cleans windshields, it removes scratches off the glass. During his little product debut party, a friend suggested he call his formula, "Windshield Swiper." The name stuck.

Picture Perfect

The first step for both companies is to take a photo. It must be a professional looking shot so if you can't do a proper job, find a professional who will do it for no more than twenty or thirty dollars. This is when it pays to have a friend who is a photo buff who can take an excellent photo for no charge.

To photograph Windshield Swiper, Mr. Adams had his local artist friend make up some labels and attached them to a couple of dummy bottles. He took a two-foot by three-foot sheet of clear white art paper. Since the bottles are a little dark, the white background will help to show up the product. His photographer curved the art paper against a corner of the wall and floor to create what is called a seamless background. When the photo is processed, all the viewer sees is the product on a white background.

If Mr. Adams wanted to get a little more sophisticated, he could also take a picture of his product in action, perhaps showing half of a scratch removed. Some products mandate a demonstration photo to make their function clear to the reader. Another advantage of the "Action Photo" is that it can get the message across more immediately.

For the Women's Work Company, the two women are currently working out of their own homes. Also it's harder to take a photo of their product. However, through their initial query releases, they already have one small client who has a very modern-looking office.

They don't know any photographers, but they found an easy way around that one. One of the local papers has assigned a photographer to take a picture of them in their client's office. He has agreed to give them the full use of this excellent photo if they will promise to keep him in mind if ever they produce a major ad for a client or themselves.

Get the picture? You want a 3" x 5" glossy photo that the publications may enlarge or decrease. Generally your release will entail a few inches in a single column, but sometimes, you'll luck out and get much more space. You need thirty clear copies, or the magazines won't run them. The least expensive copies are attainable at any photo-reproduction service who can make copies much cheaper than a photographer can. We are aiming to save money, but we never want to look sloppy or disorganized.

All in a Word

Next, we need to tell our readers what we're talking about. Dig out those original releases you submitted during your initial test phase. I assume they are in the form of a newspaper or magazine clipping. You can see that the various publications have usually modified and cleaned up your original literary gem.

Read the press releases in your collection of trade magazines. Get an idea of their style and layout. Get out your pen or tape recorder and rehash that release. Our fictional Mr. Adams has chosen his action photo to work with. Though he received some positive feedback from his original releases, he wasn't very pleased with how they were rewritten by the publications. Here's what they did:

> *"Adams Reliable Auto Products, Inc. of Worcester, MA, claims to have developed a product that supposedly removes scratches from windshields. For further information, write Adams Reliable Auto Products, P.O. Box 75, Worcester, MA."*

"Claims?" "Supposedly?" What kind of help is that? The first time, most publications gave him only a couple of inches of space, at most. This time around, his releases are playing much better. Here's how most of them now read:

> *"Adams Reliable Auto Products, Inc. of Worcester, MA, introduces their new Windshield Cleaner/Scratch Remover. As seen in the photo, the product, called WINDSHIELD SWIPER is one of the first ever to completely remove deep windshield scratches. After the scratch is removed, the glass is left completely clear and in tact. For further information, circle #85 on the reader-response card, or write Adams Reliable Auto Products, Inc., Box 75, Worcester, MA or call....(include phone number!)."*

He did five things differently this time. First, he sent a photo. Then he learned how to sharpen his description of Windshield Swiper. Then how did he get the magazine to eliminate the cynical wording? Very simple. He sent them a professional sample. The magazine had the time to try it out and see it work. As an added bonus, they also gave him a reader-response card number just for the asking.

In addition, he discovered that the magazine had a toll-free number so he called them to discuss his product. Generally, you won't have to go through all these steps to ensure a good release. Still, it's nice to have these means available to you.

It's not going to be feasible for many of you to send a sample of your product. Instead you can send any performance tests or even testimonials from credible sources. For a service entity like Woman's Work, they have only one client but they have boosted that client's profits by thirty-five percent.

The women asked their client to write a brief letter attesting to this increase and included copies with each release request. Don't worry if you have no samples or testimonials to send. For the most part, unless your claims seem ridiculous, your release will run in a positive light. Whatever you do, you should include with your release a cover letter on your letterhead. We would recommend the following format:

Date (Important)
(Addressee)

Dear (name of press release person, if available):

My company is pursuing viable avenues of results-oriented advertising and your magazine was recommended to us. I would appreciate if you would run this press release and photo in your upcoming issue. If you have any questions regarding the information I have sent you, please call me at your earliest convenience.

Thank you very much for your prompt and courteous attention.

Respectfully yours,

(Your name)
(Your title)

---

4) Get Your Message Placed

You should now be well on your way to assembling your complete packages for your target publications. Your new packages should pack a lot more punch than your initial queries. Some of the magazines will still chop and modify, but that's perfectly okay.

If, however, they inform you that they charge a small service fee to place your release, cross them off your list for now. You are offering these magazines an opportunity to grow with your venture. If they're not perceptive enough to comprehend that, then their business acumen is highly limited.

Connection #13
Sending out Your Package

In keeping with our theme of "Move Forward or Rot," let's begin our advertising campaign. You've lined up your thirty magazines. Don't short change yourself on the number. We're just barely getting by with thirty. During the Olympics, we had product releases in over eight hundred magazines.

List #1

Go over your list of publications and choose six that you feel will have the greatest impact. With the balance of magazines, choose three each of your consumer, trade, and general newspaper publications, nine in total. Of these nine, one should be from your high impact list. Label this as list #1.

List #2

Repeat this procedure with another nine magazines, except this time, choose two others from your impact list. This is list #2.

List #3

You should have twelve publications remaining, which include the remaining three from the high impact column. This is list #3.

Buy thirty 5" x 7" (approx.) top-folding envelopes. The larger size is used for more than just the purpose of accommodating your photo.

Within each envelope, be sure to include:

- ❏ Your cover letter and news release on your business letterhead. Each cover letter may be a photocopy or offset printed, but you should affix your original signature on each one.
- ❏ Your product photo, with your business card taped to the back.
- ❏ Any additional supporting documentation, with your business card stapled to each document.
- ❏ A piece of cardboard to protect the photograph.

If you're able to mail an actual sample, be sure to include the above package in your sample mailing. Don't send your sample unless it appears completely professional and refined. Get help from your local starving artist or printer, or both. If your product looks and photographs sloppily, that's tantamount to the guest of honor attending a formal gathering in a torn shirt and old blue jeans.

If your product presents itself well, but you haven't developed a container yet, at least seal it in a sealed plastic bag. When I first began shipping out product samples, I didn't have a plastic bag sealer, so I used to go to my local meat market. For a few bucks, they would professionally heat seal all of my wares—and never did anything smell of sirloin.

Don't let anything arrive damaged. Protect it well, if only with newspaper. Mail a couple of test shipments to yourself to see how your packaging holds up.

Address each package or envelope and always use a specific name, if available. To the lower left of the address, write the word, "PERSONAL" as shown below—space and underline each letter.

Your Name
Your Address

                      Name
                      Address

P E R S O N A L

If a specific name is unavailable, head the address with: Attention: News Release Department. Off to the lower left of this address, write: "DATED MATERIAL ENCLOSED. PLEASE OPEN IMMEDIATELY."

Your Name
Your Address

Attention: News Release Department
Address

DATED MATERIAL ENCLOSED.
PLEASE OPEN IMMEDIATELY

Gather up your mailings from list #1 only, march on down to the post office and send them off regular postage. The post office should be adequate for most of you unless your parcel weighs enough so that a parcel service could ship it cheaper.

If you can afford the extra dollar or so, send each mailing certified mail. Though not mandatory, this type of mail can often command more immediate attention and response. Overnight mail is also highly effective if your budget allows.

Those first nine mailings should have been fairly painless on your budget. If you've followed our instructions your initial releases should begin appearing within the next two months.

After five weeks from your first mailings, send off your mailings from list #2. Five weeks after that, mail off to all your addressees on list #3.

Connection #14
Follow-Up for Success

Back to your first mailings which are now hurrying off to their respective destinations. When we carry out publicity programs like these, nearly everything we send gets published. That's what happens with a few years of experience. When we started out, less than half of our items were published. If we had known all of the things we've shown you in this chapter, our response rate would have been much higher.

After your first mailings, do nothing for about one week. On the following week, call those magazines who have a public access toll-free number. To find most toll-free numbers, dial 1-800-555-1212. There are also many free toll-free directories available or a CD-ROM directory for a nominal cost.

When you call these magazines, ask them if they have received your news release and then find out when it may be published. If they need something else from you, do what you can to accommodate them, outside of paying any fees for your releases. Through these phone calls, they may find you and/or your product interesting enough to write a small article. Generally, each magazine will have a schedule revealing when they will be publishing various topics. Find out if there is a specific issue that may be ideal for the release of your product.

Directories and More Directories

Many publications produce industry-related directories. These directories list all sources relevant to that industry. Often, you can get your product or service listed in these directories for free, and under many different sub-headings.

And don't forget catalogs. B. Klein Publications of Coral Springs, Florida sells an excellent directory listing 9,000 mail-order catalogs. There are other excellent directories also available electronically.

Often these directories and catalogs are free for the asking, especially if a publisher is trying to promote it to the industry or the general public. If that's not possible, sometimes they will send you a previously published issue for free. It is important to note, however, that some publishers frown upon sending out old issues because some of the information may be obsolete. What have you got to lose by asking?

All of these gratuities are really not mere giveaways. They represent an investment on the part of the various publishers in your venture as well as the future of their industry. Such investments are the kind of premiums that can really pay off for a publisher as your endeavor grows. There is always the other side to contend with. Some of you will be flatly told that no releases are accepted or that your release will be subject to a several month waiting period.

The waiting period is no problem. Just try to get an idea of your publication date and then change over the name of this publication onto list

#3. Then pull another publication off of list #3 and send it off immediately. If they seem negative on any free news releases, be very courteous and thank them for their time. Why be kind to people who will scarcely give you the time of day? The reason should be obvious. You need to make good friends in your field and you never know when your paths may cross under very different and far more affluent circumstances.

In my years of being involved in the product-end of marketing, there is one salesman in particular for whom I have a tremendous admiration. He is Grady Reed, who you shall learn more about later. Grady started with nothing but a willingness to learn and a drive to survive with superior vision and integrity.

Grady is keenly aware that presenting himself as a decent human being is as important as the product he is selling. He aims to make friends, which keeps doors open.

So if the outcome isn't positive at first, if all parties involved deal with the problem responsibly and with good character, the result can pave the way to very strong future friendships and positive business relationships.

Keep that friendship factor in mind, but remember that we always try to find alternate routes leading towards our intended goal. If a publisher initially gives you the cold shoulder, wait a few days or a week and then call back. This time, ask to speak to the advertising salesperson.

Tell this person why you sent your information to the magazine and what it could mean if your press release is successful. Often times, a perceptive ad salesperson will invest a few column inches to pave the way for positive dealings in the future.

If all else fails, find out what type of editorial material they will accept and submit a small article. In the meantime, some of you may have received notes or phone calls from the various magazines. These first nine releases will give you some excellent experience on how to get your best releases out there.

It is advisable to have a few extra release packages handy in case a magazine misplaces it or if you find additional publications that you want to be in. As you get ready for your next mailing, there may have been some changes in your product. Modify your news release accordingly and send them away!

Your third mailing at the end of your last five-week interval should be your best. Some of your first releases should have appeared by now and you can use those releases to further perfect your presentation.

Most of you will enjoy a good degree of success with this major kick-off of your advertising campaign. Your net result is actually a cornucopia of benefits generally reserved for publicity campaigns costing several thousands of dollars.

With the help of the next chapter, you will learn how to deal with questions that can really make your jaw drop. What if a company wants to buy ten gross of your product? Who do you send samples to? What about quantity discounts and payments? What about brochures? And most importantly, how do you close the sale?

The above questions are known as "Demand Problems" and they are the best problems in the world to have. For thousands less than what is conventionally spent in advertising today, you could be on your way to a real fortune. Whatever happens now, at the very least, you know that you can feasibly take any good idea and give yourself a chance to profit handsomely without having to gamble away large sums of money.

The price of making a good dream happen is good thinking, not big money! In simplest terms, you are all seeking to develop a concept of the highest integrity and then connect with the right seller, distributor, etc. and the right buyer. But again, most people don't even stop to think about who their best prospective audience might be.

5) Focus on Your Audience

Bull's-Eye Neglect

This is such an ironic malady because a prospective buyer is generally known as a *target* or target market. Most people are only familiar with the term *target* as it pertains to shooting something. We don't just shoot an arrow in the air, we aim for the bull's-eye and we concentrate our energies on reaching that target. Yet in product or service marketing, too many people don't even look for their target market. Instead they try to sell to just about anybody without even aiming, and of course, usually run out of arrows before they hit their target.

Connection #15
Identify Your Target

So, if you haven't guessed, our first task is to identify your target audience(s). Where are they? Who are they? Use the form below:

Prospect Profile

Describe
Concept: _____

_____

_____

_____

_____

What will the concept be used for? _____

_____

_____

_____

_____

Where are similar concepts used and sold? _____

_____

_____

_____

What places might my relevant audiences visit for recreation?_____

_____

_____

_____

For education? _____

_____

_____

_____

For shopping? _____

_____

_____

_____

What types of relevant newspapers, magazines, newsletters might my prospects read?

_____

_____

_____

TV or radio? _____

_____

_____

_____

Now you have a target—something to aim for and hone in on, and suddenly your world of prospects seems far less overwhelming because you have a fairly good idea of what you're aiming for.

"But Where Do I Get My Bow & Arrow?"

While we may be closer to reaching our target, knowledge of where you want to go doesn't get us there. You have to learn the tricks of your particular trade—the inroads to your market.

Why Not Just Hire a Distributor?

Engaging the correct distributor or sales representative (a distributor generally buys then distributes your product to specific retail markets; a sales representative may generally act as a broker for many different companies) can be a component part of your plan but certainly doesn't guarantee mass sales. There are plenty of distributors and representatives out there, but many serve only a fraction of a particular market. You have to find the one who can reach your market. Then you still have to call attention to your concept.

Support

Assuming you go with a distributor, you still have to figure out how people are going to know your product is available. Maybe you'll need several distributors. It's all part of the search. But to reach a market successfully, you have to address several aspects of marketing and each aspect should work in concert with the other.

Just as we have undertaken everything else in a progressive test-step format, this will be most important when it comes to advertising. Most people have a very narrow vision of what advertising is. They think it means buying space in a publication or some other form of media, after which time, people flood to the stores and buy like crazy. If that were true, every venturer would simply buy ads and just cash in.

Of course, successful exposure is really a very different story. You have to focus, then your production has to make the right impression and you have to be frugal to protect your investment and maximize your return potential.

Summary

1) Understand How Advertising Really Works

- ❏ Be credible.
- ❏ If you are going to use an advertising agency, do your homework so agencies can't prey on your ignorance.

2) Identify Media Targets

❑ Complete Connection #12 to locate appropriate publications for your news releases.

3) Create a Professional Image

❑ Create a business name if you haven't already.
❑ Create a complete business correspondence look, i.e., business cards, letterhead and envelopes.
❑ Acquire a good photograph.
❑ Write credible product or service descriptions.

4) Get Your Message Placed

❑ Submit news release packages as outlined in Connection #13 and according to the prescribed timetable.
❑ Make sure you follow-up—see Connection #14.

5) Focus on Your Audience

❑ Make sure you are focused on the right target audience—see Connection #15.

Potential Challenges and Solutions

Challenge: Can't locate the right special interest publications.

Solution: This is very unusual. We have never known of a product or concept that didn't have a related publication of some sort. You need to carry out better homework.

Your local librarian should at least be able to point you in the right direction. Make certain you have checked out any related industries or retail businesses. Try the Yellow Pages.

Check the newsstands and ask the magazine stores if they can look up your related topics in their order books.

Challenge: Can't get anything published.

Solution: Seek out additional magazine sources. Find out why your items have been rejected and make the proper corrections.

For any aspect of our society, there's a form of media that represents it. Stretch your imagination. Get your news out there.

Before You Continue...

❑ Have you researched potential publications for free exposure?
❑ Have you written energetic press-releases that clearly communicate the advantage of your concept?
❑ Have you followed our procedures for submitting?

Chapter Ten

Credible, No-Risk Paid Advertising
Crossovers, Coupons and Cuts

> *"He who has a thing to sell and goes and whispers in a well, is not so apt to get the dollars, as he who climbs a tree and hollers."*
>
> **From the back of a sugar packet from Kraft Foods, at D'Olympio's Deli in Hyannis, Massachusetts**

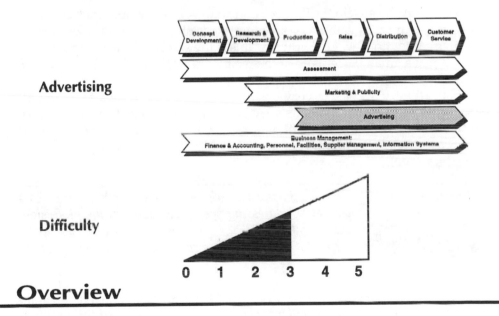

Advertising

Difficulty

Overview

We are going to further explore how to transform advertising from an out right risk into a viable investment. There are unlimited free or low-cost means to gain high-integrity exposure for your efforts.

Action Steps

1) See advertising as an investment.
2) Place media creatively.
3) Put it all together.

1) See Advertising as an Investment

You grab your mail and there it is—a windowed envelope with a check for five-thousand dollars in your name. Completely surprised, you drop everything to open it. This money's really going to come in handy.

Hopes immediately fade as you behold the entire document which says, "Imagine if you saw the following in the mail." This is followed by the now obvious dummy check, but it's too late. You fell for it. You opened the envelope before throwing it away.

What about the envelopes that congratulate you for winning a free TV, or the ones that warn you that your big prize is about to be canceled. Direct mail organizations will tell you that this is the state of the art for the medium. If just a small percentage of the recipients respond, the effort pays off.

This is all very good and very bad. What's good is that we all love getting gifts of some sort. What's very bad is that the deceit makes us very bitter and mistrusting. We feel invaded, and an increasing percentage of us are growing so numb, we are probably throwing away some real checks as well.

My father-in-law is a prominent obstetrician/gynecologist who has composed a  *newsletter addressing specialized cases in his profession. Traditionally, OBGYN's submit complicated case questions which the publisher sends to various specialists to answer.*

In the past few years, the responses began falling off sharply. When followed up on, most of the potential respondents claimed they never received the questionnaires.

Actually, they had, but the return address had only the publisher's name on it. Most thought it was junk-mail so the stuff never made it in the house. Then they began using my father-in-law's name on the envelope and guess what? The doctors are responding again.

There are ways you can do mailings and other media placement, with little or no money up-front, but even if you learn what they are and how to do it, how can you determine the ones your audience will respond to?

The primary answer is to test with as minimal financial risk as possible. We've already worked on getting an understanding as to how to profile our prospective target. Now you have to take that one step further and develop a calculated sense of where your audience is. Here's a good example from the Bronson Scrapbook:

A few years back, I had written a couple of bereavement books. The first one, Early Winter, received outstanding initial reviews but had lousy sales. It was well-packaged, attractive and highly recommended, yet somehow no campaign proved viable.

Then one day I caught a national talk-show hosted by Joy Brown, the 'tough-love' psychologist. I had a hunch that my audience was there; people actively looking to heal. The national network liked the 'fit' of the idea and agreed to run a two-month test, whereby they received $5.00 for each of my books they sold through their ads. The campaign worked and Early Winter, followed by its sequel, Winter's Passage, became almost overnight hits with consistent referrals and 'sell-throughs' ever since.

So the first rule of thumb is to find your audience. What are they watching, reading or listening to? If you're close to your target, you'll create the potential for a mutually profitable formula between your enterprise and that media.

Next, based upon the logic of the profit potential, you'll need to convince that magazine editor, radio or TV station, network sales-manager, etc., that your enterprise represents, at the very least, a good bet for a market-test. Very often, especially the smaller stations or publications will want to work with you and will even help you to develop a no-risk test, since they know that their real profits are based upon sustainable client relationships.

They will also often help you write and produce your ad for no charge because they know that if the ad is produced properly, your concept will have the best chance of selling.

Honesty is Best, but Attention for that Honesty is Better

As exemplified in the previous paragraphs, there are always innocent victims for every form of outright media deceit. It's enough to make the average entrepreneur wonder about media credibility in general. So how do you get people to respond without having to mislead them to gain their attention? The positive avenues available could fill volumes. We discuss more about copywriting in Chapter 12. Be clever, witty, bright and effective and always, always get expert opinions on your writing. Be substantive and don't lie because that will always come back to haunt you.

The underlying premise must be honesty. You can give away gifts, specials and discounts. You can advertise this to a limited extent on the envelope of a direct-mail package. But never orient your copy so it seems to promise something that you can't really deliver. First of all, it's generally illegal and secondly, your quick fix can chew away at your credibility.

2) Place Media Creatively

Mass Mailing Blues?

If you ever carry out a direct-mail campaign and receive a similarly low response rate, don't let anyone convince you that you should be satisfied with a low response rate. What you should be considering is that you're not focusing sufficiently on your audience.

Perhaps you have a good retail-use product or service and you're convinced that an honest mass-mailing campaign is the way to go. Should you invest several thousands to undertake a direct-mail campaign? You could wind up spending a lot of money just to turn sour on advertising. Proceed with caution and don't expect any miracles from a mass-mailing, unless your target has either previously purchased from you or is given great incentives.

If you really think a mass-mailing will best serve your cause, try utilizing the following two money-saving tips:
1) Instead of laying out the cost of all that postage, if applicable, see if you can pay your local newspaper to distribute your brochure as an insert.
2) Include in your brochure a discount coupon just to introduce yourself. Direct-mailing always has a better chance when you give people a real incentive to respond.

Ad Specialty Items

There is a fantastic multi-billion dollar industry known as the "Ad Specialty Industry" or "Remembrance Advertising." The beauty of this industry is that it creates, manufactures and sells gifts of virtually any product with the name, address or slogan of a business firm imprinted on the product. Since specialty items are generally sold in large quantities, they are usually low-dollar products but there can be exceptions. Maybe you could approach corporations to utilize your product as an ad specialty.

Crossovers

Crossovers or specials or premium offers essentially permit you to hitch a ride on a widely distributed product. You see these offers everywhere, everyday—"Special Offer," "Free Offer"—on cereal boxes or any product. Relevancy is the key. Seek out widely distributed products that might already be attracting your potential customers. Your product or service must somehow compliment, but not compete with your piggyback targets.

Suppose you produce a video tour-guide of Cape Cod. Ocean Spray juices are largely a Cape Cod product. You could approach them to make a special offer of your video on some of their products. Maybe to buy your video at a special discount, the customer must include two proof-of-purchase seals from two different bottles of juice.

In theory, Ocean Spray should love it because it increases consumer interest for their product. You really love it because your product is advertised in millions of homes for a longer period than your direct mail might have been, all at tremendous savings.

You could develop reciprocal coupon or discount agreements where the two products each offer a discount on the other. The options are as extensive as there are products and services, then multiplied by each other in all combinations. What an opportunity to get it out there.

Maybe a travel magazine would co-op with you and offer your video to every new subscriber. There's no limit to whom you could approach, Win-Win. Everyone benefits, and once again you've carried out exposure for your goods or services for little or no money or risk.

TV Direct Response

What about those "Isn't That Amazing" direct response TV ads. Sometimes, these work quite well, especially if a small TV station is willing to take a percentage of your profits in lieu of an ad fee. Maybe they'll do the same for your conventional ads. You never know until you ask.

Game Show Prizes?

Some popular TV game shows are seeking out particular consumer products as prizes. For little or no fee, your product could get national exposure. What have you got to lose by simply asking?

Responding to the Rush

What about fulfillment and supply? What if you get thousands of orders for your product? We maintain that demand problems are the best problems to have. Don't prepare by overstocking, but instead have resources ready should you need to switch into high gear. You'll find the fulfillment solutions. Just be sure to always work within the time frames and commerce laws governing shipping and response times.

3) Put It All Together

You don't need a degree or license to employ these techniques as your own, just like you don't need to waste money on marketing techniques that do nothing but leave you with less money. We want you to have the success without having to spend to excess.

If you've followed our advice up to this point, you have given your idea a chance without wasting a lot of money. You can see that our greatest emphasis has been on three basic aims:
1) Free news and new product releases through print sources including wire services.
2) Free distribution and exposure through crossover promotions and 'per-inquiry' arrangements.
3) Free exposure through game shows, TV shows or other public events.

There are many marketing books available, all packed with an encyclopedia of advertising techniques. That has not been our intention with this book. We feel that you will best benefit by utilizing the specific techniques outlined as a general format. Advertising that does not promote sustainability and long-term sales growth may profit a station or magazine in the short-run but will not build the important profitable long-term relationships that all vested parties need for viable growth.

Look around you. There's advertising everywhere. You see glimpses of products on TV shows, movies, local bike races, fundraisers; all promoting name-recognition, goodwill, and hopefully that appropriate spark to motivate the consumer or end-user to act. And as many ways as there are to advertise, there are twice as many arrangements to pay for that exposure; many of which cost either nothing up front or nothing at all.

How does your idea fit in the world? Where are the exposure possibilities that you can create when you're not there to sell it first hand or to the masses? How can you create arrangements that will profit your enterprise, especially in the beginning when it's most needed?

Virtually every venture needs to be marketed and advertised, and in advertising, it's generally an accepted prospect that you risk money for possible return, especially with new ventures. Hopefully, through this chapter, you should begin to see that you don't have to do it that way and that advertising and general exposure can become the viable investment that it was meant to be.

Summary

1) See Advertising as an Investment

❑ Know your audience.
❑ Develop your ad.
❑ Be honest.

2) Place Media Creatively

❑ Be creative about mass mailing.
    ❑ Investigate newspaper flyers.
    ❑ Provide a coupon with your offer.
❑ Approach relevant businesses about ad specialty items.
❑ Find a related product you can approach for a piggyback mailing.
❑ Explore all exposure and distribution avenues that can display your product without draining your bank account.
❑ Try direct response TV ads, especially if you can share profits with the station in lieu of an ad fee.
❑ Investigate placing your product as a game show prize.
❑ Be prepared to respond to a rush.

3) Put It All Together

❑ Try all of the approaches we have laid out for you.
❑ Look at what others are doing and learn.

Potential Challenges and Solutions

Challenge: Getting discouraged about making a good piggyback distribution contact.

Solution: Never pin your hopes on just one or two possibilities or you'll be a slave to their requisites. Try to create ten viable options for each program.

Even if a company rejects your idea at first, find out what changes you could make and resubmit.

Challenge: Can't find any piggyback distribution possibilities.

Solution: Finding the right one can take some time. This chapter tries to scratch the surface of piggyback options available to you. New systems pop up every day.

Before You Continue...

❏ Are you now exploring ways to make advertising work for you by means of free exposure?
❏ Have you identified specific exposure ideas that best suit your venture?
❏ Have you followed through sufficiently to enact your campaign?

Chapter Eleven

Publicity
Winning Sales by Earning Hearts

> *"Success is closely tied in with the extent to which you serve others."*
>
> **Reverend Bruce Miles**

Marketing and Publicity

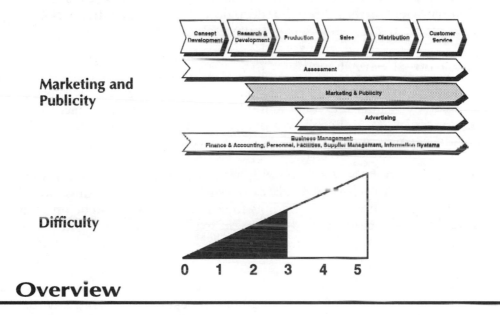

Difficulty

0 1 2 3 4 5

Overview

If you could achieve more credibility and results with a virtually free, well-strategized publicity campaign, wouldn't that be the wisest way to begin? As an added plus, the benefits often extend far beyond your original concept.

Action Steps

1) Understand the importance of genuine goodwill.
2) Build an image from the beginning.
3) Make the goodwill mutually profitable.

1) Understand the Importance of Genuine Goodwill

"Full Spectrum Marketing," "Saturation" and "Market Penetration" are just a few of the terms used for the art and science of successfully getting a message out. You must do more than reach a target (intended) audience. You have to motivate them to act positively on your message. Think of how many billions of dollars large corporations spend just to get you to like them, even if you sometimes want to hate them. Corporate image—how often companies lie and how fortunate that you won't have to. You're going to prove that you really care about your community and the worthy causes that your potential customers care about, not just on the surface but deep down and consistently, so choose your causes not just strategically, but wisely as well.

The Truth about Advertising

In general, the advertising professionals will cut one another's throat to win you over. Take a moment to think how much advertising has affected your own life. You can't be too fat, thin, ugly or handicapped unless an advertising campaign develops ethics of convenience for profit's sake.

It doesn't have to be that way, and you can still create successful, very low-cost publicity campaigns that work just as well. Advertising should and can be much more of a credible force in our society. You begin with a quality product or service. Then you tell the truth well. You prove your compassion.

The Full Spectrum

Of course, you have to deliver that honest message through many different sources (spectrums). That is why you will incorporate the various spectrums we outline, and therefore, you will increase your chances of motivating your prospects. In short, never assume that one ad, one letter or any single spectrum will achieve your desired results.

Advertising is much bigger than most of us realize. Virtually every facet of our lives is affected by it. We are just beginning to realize the great evil and great good various advertising and public relations campaigns can create. The news events and people in our day-to-day lives don't just tell us what's going on, they can change the way we look at ourselves.

So what do publicity campaigns do? They work to win your heart, claiming to be part of this fabric as well. They win your heart, they may earn your trust and loyalty.

There are no shortages of heroes in this world. The problem is that most of us don't know where to look for them, and our quest is somewhat blinded by the business of terrorism which not only holds individuals hostage but international television as well. When a handful of terrorists strike, these murderers hijack a global audience for their cause.

Broadcasters will argue that they have an expressed responsibility to deliver the news. But what happens when they inadvertently promote and enhance terrorism and related acts of horror by making TV celebrities out of the perpetrators?

In the late eighties, there was an interesting trend in national newscasting: Tears. And more teary-eyed newscasters after a sad or horrible story. That trend worked for a while, but they're not crying any more; not because there are any fewer heart-wrenching stories; it's because you're not crying anymore. You've heard it all before. You're more focused, not on other's whining but on what you can do at various levels to maintain greater global and or regional well-being.

You are more solution-oriented, and savvy advertisers realize this because they know that the real differences are made by you. That's right, you. You're going to show the world where the media coverage really belongs; not with acts of horror but with the little personal civic efforts that you can make to attack these problems. After all, who likes to see grown newscasters cry? Shouldn't the press play a more active role in reporting a solution?

In fact, there was a novel approach introduced by a news show called 'The Crusaders.' It differed in that it not only sought out hardcopy and human-interest stories, but also engaged in viable and tangible action, leading to solution. That's media at its best.

2) Build an Image from the Beginning

You are going to be part of the world's real force of heroes, and as a legitimate reward, your venture will profit. You've already proven that the individual who seeks out intelligent solutions can always find a way upward.

For Example...

Woman's Work, Inc., wanted to incorporate their civic concerns into a viable business function. They also would love to spend twenty-thousand dollars on a modest print, radio and television campaign. The problem is they only have $341 in their company bank account.

They watch the news and read all the local papers. After a few weeks of "town-watching," they have come upon a community problem that they want to do something about: child stealing and abuse.

They easily locate a couple of missing children foundations to learn various preventive techniques they can present to the young in their community. With what little money they have, they print up special "Child I.D." cards. The cards have an area for fingerprints and a photo on the front and are kept by the parents for emergency use. The women also compose a list of safety tips that they will hand out with each card. They set up an instant camera in their office and their campaign is ready to go. Now, how about a little publicity.

All that horrible, rotten news out there. Woman's Work, Inc. had one solution, and they wanted equal time. They called three local television stations, one cable station and four radio stations. They related the problem and what they were doing about it.

As a result, the radio stations each ran several FREE public service announcements. One television station turned them down, but the other two came to their office and filmed the story. Since this was a bonafide news event, both stories played on the evening news for free.

The results? Scores of children with their mothers, many of whom were interested clientele, came to their office. A couple of times while this three-week program was running, the police came by and volunteered time to help give fingerprints. The women demanded equal time with the bad guys on the media and became local heroes. They made a viable and significant contribution to the community. The legitimate fringe benefit, of course, is community trust, credibility and a well-deserved increase in business.

One positive news story can equal scores of paid ads from the believability standpoint. Woman's Work, Inc. saved thousands of dollars in advertising costs and business became so good that they will have to hire more help.

Everyone has benefited. The community is a safer place. The company realized a success it might never have had the chance to and heightened productivity has created more new jobs. The TV and radio stations have a civic duty anyway, but now their image is enhanced because they've shown their concern for the needs of the community. That's going to help their business interests.

When good solutions get equal time with the bad news, what was once a problem now becomes an opportunity. This is not mere public relations goodwill stuff, as the term is generally viewed. Our heroes have made a viable and active contribution to their community and through the way they proceeded, profitable results were immediate and tangible for all concerned.

What's the Trick?

The child I.D. program was the ideal choice for their business, and there are thousands of other community needs. The trick is to find and address a timely topic in a manner that compels all participants to depend on your office and have a potential interest in your business.

The issues of goodwill or community involvement surround us. It isn't enough that donations are tax-deductible. Someone has to channel those funds and create the proper programs for recipients. If you knew just how beneficial the right involvements were, you'd take another, far more positive view of community service.

And Another Example...

Those who know of the young Joe Kennedy, aspiring politician and son of the late R.F.K., are familiar with his efforts as head of the Citizen's Energy Corp., an organization that helps the poor keep their homes warm during the cold Massachusetts winter months. His efforts have actually saved scores of lives of people whose only fault was poverty. You have to love this man for the genuine good he is doing.

Since his organization is nonprofit and deeply essential to the community, he deserves and gets a lot of free TV, print and radio press. He has laid a foundation of goodwill and action, and if he plays his cards right, he'll become a very bright star in the Kennedy legacy.

You Can Even Save the World

Here's another and very different example: Rock and Roll music had never really been able to shake the devil image that began in the paranoid fifties. Then, along came Bob Geldof and his production of "Feed The World." Suddenly, the music assumed focus and a conscience that raised millions of dollars and saved hundreds of thousands of lives in Africa.

His incredible life saving activities have spawned similar mass-aid activities. Giving on a global scale has become fashionable. It is incumbent upon each of us to make sure this isn't just a fad.

No one's asking you to take on the world, just the part that's somehow relevant to your venture. Give the principles in this chapter a chance to work for you. Take a good hard look at your project and put this chapter to work. You'll not only enjoy a credibility that will help build your product, you could earn enormous exposure for thousands less than it might normally cost you. And you'll deserve it.

I've had a highly successful experience marketing a group of high-quality walk-  *in medical centers. They had all the most advanced physician and minor surgical services. All they needed was to get the word out, and what were those words? I determined them to be Convenience and Compassion. As a result I gave them the following slogan; "At Our Medical Centers, we don't just get you well, we treat you well."*

In the beginning phases, these centers had a very limited advertising budget but needed far more exposure than they could afford.

Accordingly, my theory was to get us involved in all vital community services, from child safety, to special health education programs. The press always responded because we were always making positive news. Best of all, the people responded, attracted initially by our compassionate image, and permanently won over once they visited us.

At one time in a town where one of these centers was situated, the local paper was doing a special magazine on drug and alcohol abuse prevention. They were selling minor sponsorships to pay for it. When they approached me, I arranged for a local radio station to do a one-hour show dedicated to the topic.

As a result, our name appeared on the cover of the magazine and we also received free radio, and even local television coverage. We became major local heroes and everyone benefited. Business again took an upward turn. Caring can be a profitable business for all concerned if structured properly. By the way, to achieve this amount of TV, radio and newspaper through standard paid advertising avenues would have cost several thousand dollars just to achieve the same exposure. Our cost for this particular campaign was only three-hundred dollars.

Even if they had ten-thousand to blow on a conventional campaign, they would never have been able to buy the credibility I gave them for three-hundred. When you just buy ads, people know you can say almost any wonderful thing you want about yourself. If, however, you carry out good deeds and work with the media properly, the people will say those wonderful things about you.

When the people draw positive conclusions about you through your good deeds, they will, in turn, trust you and support your business.

We could all stand to hear a little more good news. Think how grateful your community, state or even country will be to you for making some good news. Currently and sadly, we're primarily served by the news media only in that we are relieved that the horrors aren't happening to us, as we sit safely in front of the TV, entertained, secure, informed and (that ugly 90's concept) NON-ATTACHED. How easily the distancing afforded us via the electronic age has made us forget that each one of us can make a difference, but we each have to once again learn to mix with the world.

Over a decade ago, we saw a continued trend of deposed dictators who used to be able to run their countries at will until television exposed them to angry masses. Marcos really met his downfall the moment he lost control of his TV station to his courageous successor.

Sometimes all news seems bad and leaves us feeling helpless, but one small step to attack those problems can make all the difference in the world, especially when millions of dream-makers out there each try to do their share. Among the great fringe benefits of your own small but significant contribution is growth for your venture.

3) Make the Goodwill Mutually Profitable

In the screwy professional world of endorsements, major athletes or other celebrities push products and causes because their elevated social status creates some degree of credibility. The irony of it all is that you can do the same thing (especially now) without having to be a superhero. Just do a good deed in your community, get the media to work with you, and you'll enjoy all the hero-credibility you'll ever need.

Don't ever be afraid to approach the media with your ideas. They are in business to serve the full spectrum information and entertainment needs of the community. Enormous, result-oriented, positive exposure can be achieved by sensible use of the media. Now you know how to build that relationship.

Camera-Shy?

That's fine. Stay that way. Shyness or excessive modesty can become a great credibility tactic. Sometimes, you can remain behind the scenes all the time and let the newscasters do the work. If you do happen to get in front of a camera, be yourself and quell your fears by remembering that you have something to teach people. After a few minor experiences, you'll get used to it. As I've said all along, give yourself a chance to discover and grow with your assets.

The emphasis is on the civic event, so find a cause that you can push and use it to your advantage. Your efforts will serve as another dimension of your overall campaign.

Who says you have to be rotten and heartless to be successful. Rotten and heartless people who happen to do well financially are not successful human beings and usually wind up spreading unhappiness wherever they go. When we refer to full spectrum marketing (intelligent saturation), we must always monitor the real needs of our community.

Many years ago, when the media and money were still a mystery to me, I wrote  *my first book called Skiing Without Seeing. If you happen to see a copy around, don't buy it. It's not my most dynamic literary work. Since my early teens, my hobby has been teaching snowskiing to disabled skiers, specifically the blind. I was rarely paid for the thousands of hours I dedicated to this effort, but it was the most rewarding experience of my young life.*

I was very dedicated to it and even helped develop special techniques to give the blind more independence on the hill. The demand for ski instructors of my type grew far beyond the supply. So I wrote a book. It was released on a very small scale, as a cassette tape, accompanied by Braille diagrams that attempted to outline various skiing positions.

It was written with all the style of a barely literate young punk. In fact the best writing was from Chris Peppel, a pioneer blind skier who recorded his own introduction.

I never sought out any money to put this whole venture together. Local printers and charity groups did all the assembly. Additionally, I personally distributed the package to every blind library I could locate.

Over the months of its release, there were several articles about it and I fared much better in the newspaper than on radio because I didn't understand all the attention.

Months later, I received a letter from the White House. It was a personal letter from then President Richard Nixon, Pre-Watergate. Apparently, a friend of mine had sent him a copy of Skiing Without Seeing in my name. Nixon's letter praised my efforts in full "nice-job-son" style. Had I known more about marketing back then, Skiing Without Seeing could have made me very rich, but even though I lost money on it, the value of what I did will last forever.

Eventually I made my money on other ventures, so what's the big deal about a little delay.

Customer Input

Consider this an additional spectrum of profiting while building a better community. It comes from Grady Reed and one of his companies called "The California Cookbook Company."

It's one thing to publish, promote and distribute a great cookbook, but Reed took this several steps further. Witness his civic-minded approach.

He compiles the books himself. He develops a theme and then puts the word out for recipes. They come pouring in from housewives, school teachers, everyone. In addition, each book is complimented with a gorgeous array of spectacular culinary photographs. Most of these photos are contributed by major food companies, in exchange for a mention in the "acknowledgment" section. The contribution of recipes and photos saves thousands of production dollars. Why are people and corporations so generous to Mr. Reed? It's all in the selling.

He started with nothing but sincerity and conviction. Within a short time, the banks were sufficiently impressed with the man and his intentions and began funding his ventures. They have never been sorry, even though there were some iffy moments in the beginning.

The lesson of this chapter is to find out how you and your venture can both benefit and profit by finding your free avenues of service-oriented exposure. It's a big world with millions of possibilities. Still there is nothing more powerful than a message well delivered. Make it your message.

As your venture grows, you may find legitimate uses for various forms of conventional advertising. But make sure it works for you.

Summary

1) Understand the Importance of Genuine Goodwill

2) Build an Image from the Beginning

❑ Seek out examples in the media of promoted community services, charities, etc.
❑ Determine the community cause you can best champion with your product.
❑ Develop a plan which clearly shows you and your product aiding that cause.

3) Make the Goodwill Mutually Profitable

❑ Develop all free media avenues to publicize your interwoven cause.

Potential Challenges and Solutions

Challenge: Can't find a relevant civic project.

Solution: There are always issues that need desperate attention. Just ask your clergy, social worker or police officer.

Indeed, you want people to buy your goods or services on their own merits. Somehow your product improves somebody's life. If it's something for a handicapped person, that is ideal media material in its own right.

If your idea is a better widget with no civic relevancy, that doesn't prevent you from doing something to increase your prospects' impression of you. As the respect increases, more people will believe in what you're selling. Consider a well-publicized donation of your product to a needy group.

It's important that you are genuine with your endeavor, so find a cause you can be sincere about.

Before You Continue...

❑ Have you looked at your project from either a community or global enhancement perspective?
❑ Have you thought of ways to create positive imaging for your concept that would lead to free publicity?
❑ Have you developed some initial steps to help achieve your plan?

Chapter Twelve

Conventional Advertising
If It Doesn't Pay, You Don't Play

> *"Money is nothing more than a by-product of how you see yourself at any given time."*
>
> **Howard Bronson**

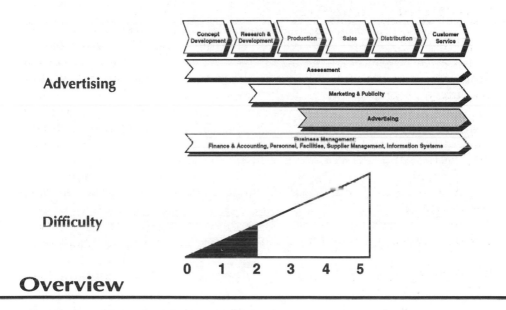

Overview

You may be very savvy, but when it comes to advertising, you are a gullible lot. When promoting a concept, it all comes down not to ego-gratification, but bottom line. Remember that the prettiest lies are always worse than the ugliest truths.

Action Steps

1) Create honest success.
2) Hire help as a last resort.
3) Structure a realistic campaign.

1) Create Honest Success

The year was 1849. It could have been any hot summer afternoon on that dusty downtown Denver Main Street if it weren't for that sound, the one that made children, mothers, cowboys and soldiers come a runnin'.

The familiar clip-clop and clanging meant only one thing. Jeremy Jonas was a comin'. His age was beginning to show as he tried to hide his strain as he set up his stage. He used to love the kids, but he doesn't even bring 'em candy anymore. "Dang kids are everywhere," he shouts. "Ladies, kindly git a hold of yer dang yunggins."

As always on his monthly visit, Jeremy began with the private sales to the bar maidens as mothers covered children's eyes. The pretties paid in cash or by "services," although these days old Jeremy preferred cash. He was getting too old and now he just wanted to take the four hundred dollars he had saved up over the years and get a ranch and stop scurrying. The biggest sales always came at the end, the one's that made him famous throughout the Southwest. The crowd swelled as Jeremy began an act he could perform in his sleep.

"Dear ladies, have you been feeling a bit extra worried lately? Is the mister not givin' you the attention he used teh? Gentlemen, are you feeling tired when you wake and even worse when you get home?"

Groans of acknowledgment spark the dank surroundings as he continued. "My dear friends, you don't have to feel that way, not if you use my miracle elixir. My special elixir isn't like any other." His enthusiasm builds as the crowd gets more excited. He's got 'em. Time to close in for the kill. "For a mere twenty-five cents, that's right, just twenty-five cents, my special tonic can work miracles for you and your family."

A voice cried out, "I'll take a bottle," followed by a sea of hands and the kind of commotion that makes Jeremy's innards smile. The noise of the crowd blocked out the rush of the hoof-beats. By the time Jeremy recognized them, it was too late.

As they grabbed him, they fired a few shots in the air to quiet the crowd. The scruffiest of the group held up a bottle of miracle elixir as he spoke, "This here miracle elixir done killed my little girl. It ain't nothing but whisky, turpentine and oil from some ol' sidewinder (rattlesnake)."

Shaking, Jeremy whispers to the man. "I've got four hundred dollars in the wagon. Let me go and it's all yours." It seemed like just a few seconds between when the noose went around poor Jeremy's neck and when the cowboy slapped the horse out from under him. This time, the mothers let their children look on.

Jeremy Would Fare Even Better Today!

Nowadays, we don't hang snake oil salesmen. Instead, we send them $19.95. Every day some advertiser finds another group of suckers. Sometimes they get caught, but most of the time, they take the money and run. We ad execs, marketers, salesmen, etc., can be a very pushy lot. After all, sales is the lifeblood for all of us and we have to survive with whatever techniques are available to us. Obviously, the bigger the package we sell, the more money we make. Yet how many ad agencies are willing to talk about the big money campaigns that didn't succeed? Believe me, that side of it is not a very glorious experience. There are many brilliant advertising people out there, but still, the only guarantees they can make are to give you their best efforts within the constraints of their own technology.

Time to bust out of those constraints. Things must change. The media must be more responsible and responsive at all levels. Even successful tycoons must rethink the massive advertising expenditures that they formerly favored simply because it seemed to work. Even for a successful campaign that costs one-hundred million dollars, what if the same powerful results could be realized for a fraction of that fee? Then companies would have more profit to expend on research, development and other high-growth areas.

And the little guy who never had the means to succeed now has those means. That's what progress is all about, a better, more efficient way that creates more opportunities and growth for everyone. We're still after great success; in fact, we're after even greater successes but at a more efficient and intelligent cost.

Stick to What We Have Taught

It's reorientation time, from that littlest inventor looking for a chance, to the great CEO's seeking a better use of communications and sales technology, and the revolution begins with each and every one of you. From now on you control your advertising expenditures, so more profit goes to you instead of people like us.

Your full spectrum marketing will cover all the angles, or pieces of the pie, to assure the success of your venture. Major agencies may push this marketing concept under many different names and their definitions can be very limited.

Full spectrum marketing has a different meaning for every venture. But for each, you must make legitimate use of every free or economical marketing technique available to you in order to reach every facet of your buying public (market).

You must also seek out useful and relevant community themes that effectively bond the various forms of media, with the side benefit being the growth and development of your venture. This chapter will give you enough of a base to understand how to separate the snake oil salesmen from the legitimate sales and marketing people. We want you to learn how to shop carefully and effectively.

Some marketing people will use this book to enhance and complement their already good techniques, so the numbers of competent advertising people are increasing daily. As the advertising industry tells the public all the time, "Why pay more?" You can ask them the same question. Why should you ever pay more for advertising that will not achieve any better results than you may now be enjoying?

Even for the least expensive venture, we have saved thousands of dollars in the birth stages during that critical first year. Still, once you've reached some semblance of cruising speed, don't feel compelled to run to the first conventional ad agency that woos you. No matter what has happened to your concept in its first year, the ad execs would have taken the profits that should have belonged to you. Even if you lost money and went down in debt and defeat, they would have made money and excuses.

There are extremely valid advertising services and agencies out there, but you must never approach them as hopeless and helpless. Our systems give thousands more ventures a chance to happen. That's better for you, and your increased successes are better for our economy. There's nothing stronger than personal excitement and incentive. No one has taken your money, spent it and left you hanging. You're too smart for that now. By employing our systems, you've given your venture a great running start, but suppose your project now mandates massive paid exposure. Though not necessarily inevitable, sometimes agency services are needed.

Barter for Ads

You may also be able to trade your goods and services for advertising time, either directly or through a third party who would accept your item and in turn, provide the advertiser with a needed service. In exchange for receiving that product or service directly from you or from another provider that you paid with your goods or services, you will receive advertising space or time.

There are folks who will make just such an investment in you, but generally, most agencies don't have that kind of faith in their results. There are definite exceptions to this type of contingency program. For example, larger agencies who maintain a staff to serve large concerns can't afford to take such risks no matter how good they are. However, there's nothing stopping that agency from trying some spot contingency programs as indicators of what could happen on a larger scale.

2) Hire Help as a Last Resort

Before you choose an agency, be certain you have gone as far as you can go using our techniques, because they do work. After several months of positive growth indicators, try recycling some of our publicity techniques. Are you continuing to build your image as a source and authority in your field? You could attempt a different angle with the magazine program or submit articles or editorials explaining (or be interviewed about) how your concept has improved things. Have you exhausted the piggyback possibilities?

Our first rule about ad agencies: Use them intelligently, only when you need them. Use wisdom in determining your advertising plans. Do not use the expenditure of high dollars as the key ingredient. You should immediately be suspicious if an ad agency:

- ☑ Insists that arbitrarily buying a large number of ads is the best way to go.
- ☑ Does not start out with comprehensive research.
- ☑ Is not willing to create a "test" relationship.

If an agency specializes in only one form of advertising, like just newspaper, what do you think they're going to tell you to do? Similarly, many radio, magazine, or newspaper advertising salespeople could approach you with the same pretense about the form of media they represent. That's a lot of what today's sales are all about. Be careful, and don't believe everything you see and hear—but you already knew that.

But don't ever believe the statistics they show you unless you can verify that they are unbiased.

Agencies should serve you when you need them to fulfill a specific task and should not create a steady draw against your profits. Larger long-term campaigns could mean an exception, but still, watch how your money is spent.

Look Closely to Tell Them Apart

If you're even considering a relationship with an ad agency, chances are you're making some money and want to make more. As you begin to realize significant profits, you'll run into two categories of business people. The first type will protect and enhance your earnings. The second type will take your money and do very little else. Keep your eyes open. We have labeled much of today's advertising as ineffective and over-weight. You, and thousands like you, are using this guide to render the dinosaurs obsolete.

Agencies currently employing the systems we have laid out will love this book, but the antiques who must now make major changes will scream loudly. That screaming is a good sign of an agency unwilling to learn and grow. Eventually and collectively, you will render this book obsolete. And then you know what will happen? With your help and feedback, we'll write a new version.

Know Your Risks and Share Them

Advertising implies risk although some agencies and systems have better track records than others. Some call this risk an investment, but how many agencies will guarantee a return on that investment?

Yes, you often have to take a chance to succeed, but sometimes agencies will take the risk with you. We generally will do so with clients as a statement of faith in our work. If an agency or ad exec really believes his or her ads will succeed, ask that person to give you a month's worth of free ads to test his promises. If those free ads work and you make money, you could consider a limited test run for a similar period of time.

Maintain the Last Word

Agencies receive fees in the form of commissions, retainers and/or salaries. Their systems of compensation vary. You also have the option of setting up an in-house agency. Or maybe you've become so proficient at your marketing, that you are all the agency you'll ever need. You hire an ad agency for one thing only—results. How they go about achieving those results varies and can make the difference between your success and failure. That's why you should have an authoritative hand in how they spend every penny.

Most importantly, if they have not read this book, you may find yourself talking way over their heads. Make sure they get a copy. Those few dollars they spend on it could make all the difference in the world for a profitable relationship with you and other successes-to-be like you.

Once they have read the book, you still must shop carefully. If you're seeking out a specific form of the media, still make sure you're only paying for what you need. Let's say you want to develop a TV ad to run on a local station, do you really need an entire agency for that? Maybe you just need a video production company or a top student from a communications college. Or maybe that local TV station can produce what you need for free or at a discounted rate since you're already buying time. If you do break down and buy ads in any form of media, make sure that particular medium gives you a healthy share of free additional P.R., news, article space, whatever is relevant to your situation. If your product does something for someone or something else, there's also a news event hiding in there.

Cut Out the Fat

When seeking out advertising services, cut out all unnecessary middlemen. Don't pay for a chain of services you don't need. A clever advertising man can advertise himself much deeper into your wallet than you really want. Shop around. As you've already seen, the exact same or better results can be realized for less if you just learn how to shop.

3) Structure a Realistic Campaign

Research Makes a World of Difference

Once you've selected an outside agency or yourself as your in-house agency, begin with research. If the agency is smart, they'll ask you all kinds of questions about you and your product, your dream. Some of the queries will seem very sophisticated, some will seem very stupid. Be patient and answer each question with respect. As they research, they are developing a proposal, which you should not have to pay for unless you execute it. The formation of a proposal or marketing plan can take a few days or a couple of months, depending on the size and scope of your venture.

Assembling a marketing proposal or plan is not a burden for a professional. The plan will also demonstrate how well that agency understands full spectrum marketing. You'll know very quickly whether they've read our book or not. Study the plan. Spend a week with it. Never make decisions right at the presentation when emotions may cloud your ability to make rational, cost-effective determinations.

Look at their fees and project what they could cost you over a year's time. Will you be locked into them even if the relationship falters? Are they taking on some of the work that you are already proficient at yourself? They may show you some artwork, slogans or body copy (the writing that comprises the ad). As you review all this material, you have to keep asking yourself, "How will this all work to sell my product?" If you're reading a lot of cute copy or medium-funny jokes, a warning flag should go up.

Beware of Humor

Humor and cuteness can work extremely well, but it requires a very special talent. Intended humor could be taken as cruel by certain groups. You can be sure that reprimands are often handed out or follies are abashedly exposed by any number of regulatory or special interest groups.

When I used to try my hand at humor with clients, I always got a kick out of myself, and generally some chuckles from my clients or prospects. There was the time I suggested the following slogan to a birth-control products company: "We Don't Deliver." It drew laughs from everyone on the board except for the women, most of whom were not amused.

To make it worse, I later learned that I was not the first with this cute pun. It then occurred to me why it's often felt that puns can be the lowest form of humor. First, they can simply be unfunny, and worst of all, many others may have already discovered that same silly phrase long before you did.

On the other hand, people eat up good puns, like the famous Skip Morrow greeting cards. The key is cleverness and originality.

Once I created a line of blue jean labels. They were cute looking things that were to be sewn over existing labels. The name of my jeans were "Who Cares." That joke worked.

One last indulgence in my own vanity regarding a hot-tub company I used to work for. As you know hot-tubs make lots of bubbles. So I made bubble gum and wrappers that read, "For Your Best Bubbles, Chew (Name of Hot-Tub

Company)." We handed them out at a couple of trade shows and they pulled in a lot of customers.

Okay, no more. I promise, except for the bandages I once made for a walk-in medical center, upon which I imprinted, "(Name of Business), Gauze We Care."

If you're feeling kind of ill right now, you understand our point about puns. If you're laughing hysterically, then we're really worried about you. Be careful with cute stuff.

Be Careful What You Say

Headlines, slogans and art are what initially attract your reader or listener. Don't lose them. As we get into copywriting, remember, don't offend people or even your competition. I know you see it done all the time from major competitors. That perplexes me because offensive tactics are remembered long after the product or message have been forgotten. If you knowingly insult people's intelligence, they'll ultimately seek revenge by losing faith in what you say. Even if they depend on your product, they'll now seek an alternative if one ever comes up. In sum, blatant offenses in any manner ultimately create new competition.

Good copywriting tells the truth in such an appealing, credible and informative manner, that the readers are motivated to buy. It's easy to stray away from that ideal since advertising and creative writing are so interrelated and multi-dimensional.

Try writing some ad copy yourself. You could be very pleasantly surprised. After all, you've already done some writing. Your magazine releases are an excellent place to draw ideas from. You can also draw from your experiences in making sales presentations. What did you say to win them over? You know your audience. Begin by writing to them just as you talk to them. Grab that trusted old friend and persuade him to believe what you're selling. Get it down on paper. A good friend will not be afraid to give you harsh criticism if you deserve it and that could prove very helpful. Whoever writes the copy, here are some additional standard pointers that they may want to integrate.

More than Academics

When new advertising students come to me they always blurt out the word, "AIDA" or "AIBA" or "AIDCM." These strange-looking words are actually letter groupings that roughly spell out the following advertising formulas:

AIDA =1. Attention
2. Interest
3. Desire
4. Action
AIBA = Same sequence with the B of Believability; or AIDCA = same sequence with a C for Credibility; or AIDCM, with M for Motivation.

In turn, we're supposed to be impressed that they can pick that up from a textbook. But can they write? Can they live with and sensitize themselves to a product and make me understand and believe what they're saying? Most importantly, can they enhance their writing from valid criticism and mistakes? If yes to all of the above, and most importantly, if their work makes money, then we don't care what formula they can recite. We are only interested in ethical, cost-effective results.

Formulate a plan. Incorporate only the professionals you really need for only the time you need them. Rework and revise that plan as you progress and discover better paths.

Power-Up Tip #7
Advertising, Marketing and Publicity:
Pulling It All Together

The chart on the next page covers many of the concepts which we have discussed in detail throughout Chapters 9, 10, 11 and 12. Use it to review and to build a consolidated advertising, marketing and publicity strategy for your *Great Idea*. Now is the time to pull it all together and make it happen if you haven't already done so. Have fun!

Blueprint for Free Advertising,
Publicity, Co-ops and Crossovers

Advertising Medium	The Wrong Way	The Right Way	Chapter
Magazines, Newspapers and Newsletters	Purchase advertising space without testing and measuring results.	Run a **Free** press release with photo.	9
		See if relevant magazine will even write an article on your venture, also for **no charge.**	9
		Keep publications apprised of any changes in your company or even staff changes, anything that maintains exposure **without cost.**	9
	Purchase national advertising in magazine or newspaper.	Advertise on the back or bottom of complimentary product in exchange for sharing profit with matching product. Cost for this is virtually **nothing.**	10
Radio, Television, Internet and other On-Line Services	Purchase advertising time on local, regional or national radio or television without identifying market targets and what percentage of market will be reached.	Make yourself or spokesperson available for **no charge to you** to the thousands of radio shows done via telephone directly from your home or office.	9
		Make yourself available for local or regional television interviews at **no charge to you.**	9
		Set up a radio or TV advertising campaign for **no money** by instead agreeing to pay station a percentage of product sold as a result of the ad.	9
		Sponsor a community service activity by providing free space or relevant product in exchange for free media exposure.	11

Summary

1) Create Honest Success

- ❏ Stick to what we have taught.
- ❏ Barter for ads as a way to save money.

2) Hire Help as a Last Resort

- ❏ If using any aspect of a conventional ad agency, make sure you know what you're buying. Pay for only the services you need.
- ❏ Begin your relationship by having the agency read this book.
- ❏ Cut out the fat.

3) Structure a Realistic Campaign

- ❏ Attempt to structure a results-oriented contingency program.
- ❏ Be sure the writing serves the need to sell the product. Beware of humor.
- ❏ Refer to Power-Up Tip #7 to review all of your options.

Potential Challenges and Solutions

Challenge: The ad people insist that the programs in this book do not work.

Solution: We would say the same thing if our livelihood were threatened.

Asking an ad exec to substantiate his discontent is not an unreasonable request. If they can give your product the same momentum and credibility in the first six months as cheaply and effectively as we can, then give them three-hundred dollars for the full six months to prove it.

By the way, prepare to say good-bye to that three hundred dollars and much more. Please don't spend more than you have to, as opposed to what they say you have to spend.

New and better ideas integrate with the old to enhance them.

You can't begin to imagine what people will promise when it comes to selling an advertising account. Let the garbage roll off your shoulders and keep your perspective. A promise is not a promise unless it is in writing and signed by the authorized and participating parties.

The advertising profession consists of persons from every imaginable profession. The only experts are those whose cost-effective techniques work for you.

If you've never met advertising people, you may be enthralled by the first one you meet. That's why you should meet several to gain the best perspective.

Before You Continue...

❑ Do you understand the realities of conventional advertising?
❑ Do you now understand how to utilize conventional advertising in a more cost-effective manner?
❑ Could you design an equally effective advertising campaign for little or no money?

Chapter Thirteen

Moving Goods and
Services to Market
The Joy of Demand

> *"Do what you can with what you have, where you are."*
>
> **Theodore Roosevelt**

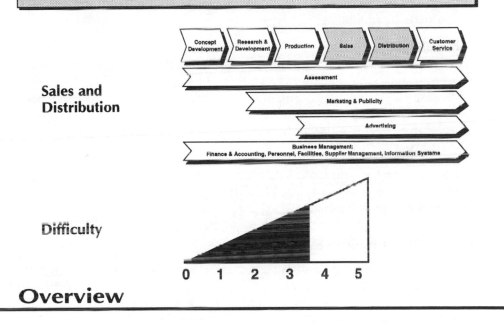

Sales and Distribution

Difficulty

Overview

This is what you've worked for—your purpose, your path and hopefully, your bread and butter. It's response time! You've cast your net;
now it's time to reel in the prospects.

Action Steps

1) Evaluate responses.
2) Be prepared with data.
3) Sound professional.

1) Evaluate Responses

When we mentioned earlier that productivity of goods and services makes money and not the reverse, we really couldn't prove that until this chapter. Your first advertising campaign is in motion and people are beginning to ask you some challenging questions. You don't want to appear ignorant because you'll be embarrassed and you'll create doubts about the integrity of your product. Letting your own doubts cause you to give up transcends foolishness. You have something that people want. That's the bottom line. Everything else between trading their money in exchange for your goods or services is secondary. You'll solve all the little headaches as necessary.

Generally you will not hear from the dry goods stores of the major retail distributors. They have a purchase and distribution system that's complex enough to write another book about. I have seen these big guys buy the small guy's products, but generally they have to be approached. Your initial advertising campaign is capable of cutting through these complexities because perceptive buyers will keep their eye on certain new product sections.

You should be hearing from a number of smaller distributors and retail dealers. They will ask you about shipping, availability, pricing, quantities, etc., and you should be ready with the answers. Make a list of all your distributor, wholesale and retail pricing information, shipping dates, everything you can think of.

There are specific terms and systems that distributors use for their specific industries. Try to learn as much about your area as you can before you make or receive your first phone call. If you are confronted with something you're not sure about, tell the truth, but tell it in such a way that won't turn off the customer. Inform your customers that you will get back to them within the week with the information.

2) Be Prepared with Data

Many will ask for price lists or brochures. Though these are generally necessary tools of the trade, aim to keep your paper exchanges down to a minimum. We have written, designed and printed hundreds of brochures and as your enterprise develops, you can do a lot of fancy things. For now, just think in terms of the "PDS" or Product Data Sheet.

This will consist of a single sheet with a black and white photograph or a very good illustration, under which you will clearly list all of your product features and benefits. This list should include product advantages over the competition, features and benefits, without revealing any secrets. Dimensions, shipping weight and quantities should also be included.

Print only one hundred product data sheets to start out with. Build up some profit and make corrections via these first hundred before you print more. You'll also need to photocopy or quickprint price lists, one for distributors, one for dealers and one for retail customers.

3) Sound Professional

When you receive calls, you can get away with simply saying "hello," but consider some alternatives. To enhance your image, you can engage an answering service who could answer with your company name, or you could use an answering machine. The easiest and least expensive route for now is to have all family members simply answer your home phone by stating your company name, just like an office line, unless your local phone system doesn't allow this.

The first time you saw your idea as something that you could touch or see function, it seemed like no excitement could ever top that. Compare that to the present as you actually respond to the demand you created. What began as a mere notion is now well on its way to improving your life and the lives of many others.

Hard work is a nice principle. We've worked hard to develop our promotional systems. No doubt that hard work has helped many people realize certain degrees of success. But nothing beats good thinking. Thus far, we've just scratched the surface of how to make your idea work. You have seen the beginnings of various avenues. There are so many more exposure techniques available to you. All you need is more of that good thinking and a willingness to not limit yourself.

Summary

1) Evaluate Responses

❑ Answer all inquiries honestly. Pledge to research what you do not know.

❏ Learn as much as you can about distribution in your product's industry.

2) Be Prepared with Data

❏ Have basic product data sheets available.
❏ Print price lists for three different audiences:
   ❏ Distributors
   ❏ Dealers
   ❏ Retail customers

3) Sound Professional

❏ Answer your phone with your company name.
❏ Consider an answering service or an answering machine.

Potential Challenges and Solutions

Challenge: No responses to your promotional campaign.

Solution: Some responses can take a few months, others will contact you right away. If most of your releases have been published and you still have received no inquiries, there may be something in your photo or your writing that's turning them off. Have you been careful to clearly portray your product as an improvement over the competition?

Give each spectrum of your campaign a chance to integrate and deliver. After all three phases of your release mailings, if things aren't at least beginning to click, reread Chapters 1 and 2. You may have missed something in concept development. Were you honest about the test results? Did you make the appropriate corrections or was your mind already made up before you began testing. Bad listening makes incomplete ideas.

Challenge: Good responses, but unsure how to handle them.

Solution: The delightful dilemma. Chances are you'll make some money under these circumstances. If just to close those first few crucial deals, hire an expert in your field on a temporary basis as a last resort.

Essentially, your prospects will be more concerned about your ability to follow-up than on a wealth of knowledge and experience.

Whatever you do, don't lose the sale.

Challenge: Overwhelmed with too many orders.

Solution: First of all, congratulations. Now don't blow it. Run to that local manufacturer and/or distributor and show them your flood of orders.

Or...many successful ventures used a garage or living room as the first office or production plant. You could develop your own fulfillment (product delivery) system and hire local high school students to help with the process.

Those orders mean money is waiting out there with your name on it.

Before You Continue...

❏ Can you respond to leads with an appropriate brochure or sample?
❏ Can you follow up properly to close the sale?

Chapter Fourteen

Business Success
The Elements of Sustained Profitability

> *"Dreams cost nothing; poor management and failure to focus on your customer can cost the dream."*
>
> **Peter Lange**

Business Management and Customer Service

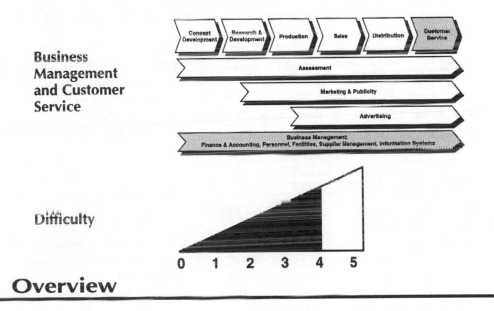

Difficulty

Overview

It has often been said that over 90% of all good ideas go undeveloped to the graves with their creators. To reverse those odds and bring an idea to life is the core theme of this book, but bringing an idea to life does not guarantee the survival and perpetuity of that idea. What's needed in the long run are sound business management practices and a focus on the needs and expectations of your customers.

Action Steps

1) Assess your business management needs constantly.
2) Take action to build management practices which will sustain your business.
3) Always listen to your customers and take action on their input.

Down in the Engine Room

Once you've created something from your heart and mind and completed the various aspects that bring it to your market, you have to engage in a major changing of hats, from creator to manager. Only children play with things for a while and then lose interest, but if your concept has truly become a part of you, and you've sustained to this point, now is the time to take the appropriate steps to eventually allow the idea to sustain you. It's time to go down into the engine room, assess the equipment you have in place to cruise your flagship and continuously monitor and upgrade engine performance to meet the demands of your market.

Most businesses tend to form themselves. Scant and casual orders for goods or services become more regulated and increased. Then one day, the house or small office space cannot possibly accommodate the calls, the flood of mail, or the necessary impression required for visiting prospects. Suddenly, what was just an idea, now becomes taxable income.

The Turning Point

Now that your dream has become reality, it's time to become increasingly realistic about building the appropriate business structure. Switching more into 'business mode' essentially becomes a function of numbers. When to set up your own office basically becomes an issue of both when space and staff are necessary and when it becomes cost-effective to obtain these resources. Being premature in building an office infrastructure can drain precious financial assets and threaten an otherwise promising idea.

One of the keys to appropriate business management is applying all logic and intuition with minimal emotion (with the exception of a positive attitude) to your managerial decisions. Don't be seduced by the trappings of a successful business until you are a successful business. Do not overcommit to space, human resources or raw materials.

As this book has evolved into your marketing plan, many of you are now formulating business plans, which generally focus on management and growth. If seeking funding or other forms of participation, don't create exaggerated promise of potential return. From the investor/participator vantage point, logical investing also begins with emotion—a sense of comfort and appeal for the idea. Sky-high projections are not the key appeal. Dreaming is safe; spending is risky. Do all you can to make sound decisions to reduce risk and increase return.

Finance and Accounting Savvy

You like your concept; they like your concept. They're buying; you're proud, but are you heading toward profit or mere ego-gratification? Using your computer or traditional ledger, it is advisable at this point to log all costs of doing business, all costs of providing goods or services, as well as gross and net profits. If you are computer wise, there are plenty of excellent PC based applications for under $50 which can help you stay on top of your finances with the smallest of effort.

If you want to free up your time for what you feel are more important matters, it is perfectly acceptable to retain professionals to assist in basic accounting tasks. However, choose wisely and be sure that you really want to spend your resources for this type of support. At some point, your venture will hopefully grow to the size that you are essentially forced into hiring professional support. At this point, assess your situation and make a prudent decision as to your course of action.

Steering the Ship

If you are in fact running the business end of your concept, the goal is to create an operation where, over time, net or actual profit after all expenses shows growth indicators after a period of two to six months, in most cases. Of course this number will vary with each venture. In that the design of this book has been to create a value-chain for your *Great Idea*, many readers have enjoyed slight revenue increases right from their initial contacts with prospective buyers.

To get to this point, many readers have become something they never have experienced in their entire lives—a leader. The issues of leadership primarily involve good ego-free listening for sound decision making, and good team building. Some of the most critical positive decisions of our time have been made by leaders who had surrounded themselves with outstanding advisors. This optimal form of decision making is called consensus; getting the best advice to then invoke the most effective and appropriate decision.

The qualifications you now possess as a leader are that you have guided your concept to this point, so you've evolved into this position. Now you have a good degree of substance behind you. Following are the key points for business success:

1) Keep the idea viable both attitudinally and financially.
2) An effective listener makes an effective leader.
3) Do not overcommit on your venture without realistic possibility of return.
4) Watch and learn from your competition.
5) Continually reassess all aspects of your venture to assure excellence and growing market share.

The Final Secret to Success

In Austin, Texas, there is a restaurant where people intentionally go to be verbally abused by the service personnel. A typical "exchange" might go something like this:

Customer: I'd like a hamburger, fries and a shake.

Order Taker: Nope, you can't have that today. Try again buddy.

Customer: Why can't I have those items? They're on your menu.

Order Taker: Forget it. I don't feel like making that today.
Pick something else or get to the end of the line.

Can you believe that people actually pay to be treated this way? Yes, if it's a gimmick, which it is in this case. But we don't want you to run your business this way.

The final secret for success which we have for you is:

Engage in ego-free listening with your customer and respond diligently, intelligently and quickly to their comments. Find a theme, even if it seems offbeat. If customers respond positively to it, that's all the proof you'll need of its efficacy.

If you have been doing this throughout your product or service development process, then you are probably becoming very successful right about now. So, keep it up. Great job! We'll be looking for you!

Connection #16
Survive-r-cise
Business Survival Exercises

> *"Our thoughts are traitors and make us lose the good we oft might win by fearing to attempt."*
>
> **William Shakespeare**

It's true. There is no gain without pain. There are no rewards without risks. However, the down sides are much easier to deal with for those who are better prepared. You will never be completely able to predict or control how the market or business trends will occur or behave. But you can, to a very great extent, control how you will deal with the unexpected and will then turn problems into new opportunities, or at the very least, part of the educational process. Please especially note that the situations depicted are not all that common or likely, but set up only as training exercises.

Following are some unusual exercises designed to help you think more creatively. There are no right or wrong answers and you may try them over and over again as time goes on. The key is to relate them to some of the day-to-day issues you will face as you gain the knowledge to build the courage to achieve your dreams. Here are the exercises and what they pertain to: One tip—try to be as creative as possible.

1) FINANCE...The Burning House

You are in the attic of an old wooden house. You are the only one in the house, and in the attic are nothing but old bed sheets and some old standard household tools. There is no telephone, no rope, nothing else.

As smoke begins to seep through the floor, you realize that the house is fully engulfed in flames and that you will not be able to escape down the burning steps, as everything below you inside the house is completely engulfed.

List at least five ways you can survive and escape:

_____

_____

_____

_____

_____

_____

_____

_____

_____

_____

_____

_____

_____

_____

_____

_____

_____

_____

2) NEGOTIATION...The Unplanned Meeting

You are at home relaxing in your backyard. Your venture is starting to make a profit, but you have still had to postpone certain bills and prioritize others to keep things going and growing.

Suddenly, a car pulls up and three tough-looking men get out and ask to speak with you. You invite them to sit with you since they are not strangers, but you never expected to see them together. One is your banker, one is your manufacturer and the third is a radio station and newspaper that you have been advertising in on a part per-inquiry/part directly payable basis.

The **banker** states that he will not lend you any more money to pay the manufacturer. The **manufacturer** informs you that he will not extend anymore credit and will not continue manufacturing until past invoices are paid and then it's C.O.D. only. Your **advertiser** tells you that he will no longer advance you any free space and that it's cash up front or no more ads.

Your product or service is selling and you need to not only maintain existing advertising, but you need to expand it.

List at least five ways you can continue the survival of your company while managing the relationships with these unexpected visitors:

_____

_____

_____

_____

_____

_____

_____

_____

_____

3) DEDICATION...The Family Squeeze

Your husband, wife, parent, whoever, is losing patience with you. Your dedication to your venture keeps you working tirelessly in the garage or living room most evenings and weekends.

But you are excited about what you're doing, and while you do agree that family comes first, you believe this venture could make a big and positive difference in your life as well as your family's. However, your spouse or friend is threatening to leave if you continue putting so much time into this. Quitting your regular job is not an option because your venture cannot possibly support you or your family at this point.

List at least five ways you can continue pursuing your concept while not sacrificing as much family time:

_____

_____

_____

_____

_____

_____

_____

_____

_____

_____

_____

Summary

Exercises are designed to stretch and condition muscles. In these exercises, we're shaping up the brain and the will. Do them diligently as they will help you to both focus and create innumerable possibilities.

Remember to:

1) Assess your business management needs constantly.
2) Take action to build management practices which will sustain your business.
3) Always listen to your customers and take action on their input.

Potential Challenges and Solutions

Challenge: I don't have the skills to solve these exercises. These require lawyers, negotiators and maybe firefighters.

Solution: It is not about skills but wills, like the inventiveness that you applied to your concept. You need to learn how to work with many different types of professionals, so reach in that brain of yours and invent new solutions, using "re-solutions."

Before You Continue...

❏ Have you survived?
❏ What uniquely special and creative steps did you take to ensure your survival?
❏ When was the last time you reviewed your mission statement?

Afterword

Our Parting Encouragement

> *"Genius, that power which dazzles mortal eyes is oft perseverance in disguise."*
>
> Henry W. Austin

Stay with It...Grow with It

"Why am I putting up with this! All I seem to get from customers is abuse and disrespect. They just don't seem to understand what my intentions are. Yet, I stay with it. No matter what, I persist, I grow, I stay with it. My friends tell me I'm crazy, but I secretly think they're a little jealous."

The above little blurb has been our thoughts many times. Even with the books we've published and the other things we've been fortunate enough to achieve, we're always having to help someone manage a crisis. And though the crises are usually ones that we've been through many times before, they are new to our clients, and we must be there, almost like a physician.

Everybody's Gotta Do Something

So why do we do this? Why do we dedicate our lives to helping dreamers succeed? Two reasons:

1) The Dreamer Is the Most Important Person in the World!

If they act upon their dream, dreamers offer new ways to do everything. New ways to live, think, eat; new ways to survive and carry on.

A lot of good ideas die unnecessary financial deaths. Or their creators first lose direction, and then the faith to continue. So we are in the survival business, and that makes our work vital and important. We like that; which leads to our second reason for doing what we do:

2) We Like What We Do!

We wake up in the morning, excited, alive and challenged, and we know that the only way to overcome those challenges is through well-directed hard work. But as hard as it gets sometimes, it's never all that frustrating because this work is an embodiment of who we are. This is our baby and we've struggled hard to make it into something. We like what we do because our work is truly a part of our talent.

Don't Quit Your Day Job...Yet.

Career changes and product development take a long time. The right direction has to be clearly recognized and strategies have to be developed.

It's like a Diet

It's really like a diet. It takes work, discipline, commitment and time. This is why, throughout our writings, we have emphasized the need to test the waters *first* before jumping in.

Your Choice

Changes can either be seen as scary or as great and exciting adventures. Every life can and should have a special meaning that can be shared. Why not pursue those things that are most meaningful to you!

TIME TO MAKE YOUR GOOD IDEAS COME TO LIFE

Each of us is born with certain gifts. The trick is to find and develop those gifts. No matter the age, social status or previous track record, it's never too late or too early to find and grow with your real talents. Percentage-wise, there are more unhappy rich than unhappy poor people. There's no greater wealth than one which stems from discovering and growing with your own natural gifts.

The first step is to discover your best ideas and then, instead of reacting to life, you can act upon your dreams.

Every idea, every proposal, every lead is completely worthless without sufficient follow-up and exploration that achieves each step of your plan. Without that follow-up, you may as well never have started in the first place.

During our formative years, most of us were continually reinforced for every effort we made. We were told that trying was more important than the results. That's fine for growing up and learning, but not for real idea-builders.

In the real world, only results count and all the empty promises delay the success that's waiting for you. It's far better to say, "I have done," than "I am going to do." Otherwise we are merely fishing for childlike gratification.

Each of you has a separate and unique opportunity to profit greatly from your dream. The more you can focus your energies on completing each step, the more you will profit.

If your concept requires meetings, make sure those meetings are creating profit. Proceed at your own pace and style, but channel your energies toward achievement.

We live in a world where the right knowledge transforms any dream into a possibility. Take this book and make your best dreams happen. Make your best self happen. Don't just wish or hope for a better world, make a better world. Let your strengths overcome your weaknesses and let yourself grow.

Our intention has been to help make all good dreams possible. That's the ideal that built this country and it's a wonderful principle.

Have we promised you instant riches like all those miracle ads that take advantage of your right to hope? Of course not! Profit motive does not forgive deceit.

Could these techniques make you rich or famous? Indeed we do have some clients who have used our techniques and become millionaires, but our goal has been to see you become more fulfillment-oriented than merely money-oriented. You could make a lot of money, but why just have things of value if you haven't developed values?

Get out there and make things better in your own way. Have fun. Maybe you will get rich. Our wish for you, however, is that this book has helped your venture give you a more enriched life.

**The sure-fire way to give your concept that special boost
needed to turn your dream into dollars!**

```
Get Lange & Bronson
on Your Team!
```

One time fee: $1,995.

Membership is strictly **limited to 350 subscribers** at any given time.

This book is a tool designed to make your idea as successful as it can
possibly be. For a one-time, annual fee, the *Great Idea! Now What?*
Network allows you to take maximum advantage of our thirty plus
years of dedicated and creative concept development.

Here are the services you'll receive:

☑ Open-line **initial intake** of your concept, available through phone,
 fax and E-mail.
☑ Critical **Full Spectrum Evaluation** and **Market Overview**, specifi-
 cally developed for your concept.
☑ Creation of your initial **press releases** for all applicable media,
 including print, radio, television and the Internet. All releases are
 written by Lange and Bronson.
☑ **Placement** of your initial press releases in both print and on-line
 services.
☑ **Unlimited written inquiries** directly to Lange or Bronson via fax,
 E-mail or conventional mail.
☑ **One hour of monthly cumulative telephone consultations** with
 Bronson and/or Lange.

This support network is comprised of a multi-faceted, action-oriented
system that provides you with customized tools developed specifically
for your concept, with the singular goal of creating maximum quality
development opportunities for your venture, for the least amount of up-
front dollar expenditure.

Conventional advertising and publicity agencies would generally charge
you up to 250% more for the same, or even less, service (we know this
because we've directed and consulted for many of these agencies). Our
system is ingeniously designed to provide you with superior service guaranteed to deliver the same or better results, but at a fraction of the cost.

Join the *Great Idea! Now What?* Network

Who Belongs to the Network?

High-tech, low-tech, upscale or no scale, the *Great Idea! Now What?* Network will deliver for you in a uniquely powerful, creative and cost-effective way, delivering the kind of results you won't find at 10 to 20 times the cost! That's the *Great Idea! Now What?* Network. Join now and let the network work for you!

❏ YES! I want to join the *Great Idea! Now What?* Network. Please enroll me as a member today. Enclosed is my check (or money order) for $1,995 to start my membership immediately. I understand that my membership is for one year from receipt of this enrollment form. At the end of one year, I can choose to enroll again for more support or free up my membership for another member. I also understand that upon receipt of my enrollment and check, I shall be contacted by telephone for initial welcome briefing and intake.

Name:_____ Company:_____

Address:_____

City:_____ State:_____ Zip:_____

Phone: _____ Fax:_____

Best Time to Call: _____ Time Zone:_____

Mail your check payable to *Great Idea! Now What?* Network and mail with this enrollment form to:

📧 *Great Idea! Now What?* Network
775 East Blithedale Avenue
Suite 216
Mill Valley, CA 94941-1565
Fax: (415) 388-8702

or E-mail your information to:

💻 Howard Bronson - HBMAN@AOL.COM

💻 Peter Lange - PWDUDE@AOL.COM

Grow Your Business With These Small Business Books From Sourcebooks—

Mancuso's Small Business Resource Guide by Joseph R. Mancuso
The ultimate directory of small business information. The perfect desktop reference!
208 pages, ISBN 1-57071-066-X (paperback)

The Small Business Legal Guide by Lynne Ann Frasier, Esq.
The critical legal matters affecting your business. Includes actual agreements and forms.
176 pages, ISBN 1-57071-060-0 (paperback)

Real World Customer Service by Bernice B. Johnston
Word-for-word ways to handle customer complaints and give superior service every time.
144 pages, ISBN 1-57071-0-62-7 (paperback)

Mancuso's Small Business Basics by Joseph R. Mancuso
Learn how to choose your business venture, raise capital, and manage for growth.
208 pages, ISBN 1-57071-076-7 (paperback)

Your First Business Plan, 2nd Edition by Joseph A. Covello and Brian J. Hazelgren
Learn the critical steps to writing a winning business plan. Includes complete sample plan.
152 pages, ISBN 0-942061-44-6 (hardcover) • ISBN 1-57071-044-9 (paperback)

Smart Hiring by Robert W. Wendover
Everything you need to know to find and hire the best employees.
200 pages, ISBN 0-942061-57-8 (hardcover) • ISBN 0-942061-56-X (paperback)

The Small Business Start-Up Guide by Hal Root and Steve Koenig
A surefire blueprint to successfully launch your own business. Includes state requirements.
152 pages, ISBN 0-942061-70-5 (hardcover) • ISBN 0-942061-67-5 (paperback)

Getting Paid In Full by W. Kelsea Wilber
Collect the money you are owed—every time—and develop a successful credit policy.
144 pages, ISBN 0-942061-71-3 (hardcover) • ISBN 0-942061-68-3 (paperback)

How To Sharpen Your Competitive Edge by Don Reynolds, Jr.
Discover keys to successfully edging out the competition and establishing market position.
200 pages, ISBN 0-942061-73-X (hardcover) • ISBN 0-942061-72-1 (paperback)

How to Get a Loan or Line of Credit by Bryan E. Milling
A banker show you exactly what you need to do to get a loan.
152 pages, ISBN 0-942061-46-2 (hardcover) • ISBN 0-942061-43-8 (paperback)

To order these books or any other of our many publications, *please contact your local bookseller* or call Sourcebooks. Get a copy of our catalog by writing or faxing:

Sourcebooks, Inc.
P. O. Box 372
Naperville, IL 60566
FAX: (708) 961-2168

Thank you for your interest!